The Town of Cambridge

A. Pugin delᵗ   J. Hill sculpᵗ

ST SEPULCHRES
The Round Church.

London Pub.ᵈ May 1·1814, at 101 Strand, for R. Ackermann's History of Cambridge.

The Town of
CAMBRIDGE
A HISTORY

BY

Arthur Gray, M.A.

Master of Jesus College, Cambridge

CAMBRIDGE
W. Heffer & Sons Ltd.
MCMXXV

LONDON AGENTS:
SIMPKIN, MARSHALL, HAMILTON,
KENT AND CO., LTD.

PRINTED IN ENGLAND

Preface

THIS work, planned and more than begun in 1913, was laid aside in War time, and was only taken up again in 1923. It has grown in scale since its inception, and many new fields of enquiry have opened themselves in the interval.

The research has proved far more interesting than at first I supposed it likely to be. For Cambridge is a town unique in its interest. That interest does not lie in association with great national events; of such it is delightfully destitute. There are towns and cities far more famous in English annals. *Laudabunt alii :* their splendour is reflected, as the moon's, or, it may be, is occasional, as that of a new sun. If Cambridge town has never been a particularly bright star in the firmament of History, its light is intrinsic, and it has shone pretty steadily for more than a thousand years. And, to complete the simile, I hope that I have succeeded in showing that it has the peculiar interest of a binary star and is not a mere satellite subordinated to the University.

The wealth of material, ancient and recent, at the disposal of the narrator is almost an embarrassment. To deal with it adequately would require a far larger volume than this. In footnotes I have acknowledged my obligations to some of my predecessors in this field. One of them is not so recognised—the writer whom Professor Maitland called 'our great town clerk,' C. H. Cooper. I have not thought it needful to state my particular indebtedness to him, for it would have to be repeated on nearly every page. Since the publication of his *Annals* sources unknown to him have been explored, and I may claim to have added a good deal of my own to the stores that my predecessors in print have accumulated. Among those predecessors I have gathered much from the admirable *Township and Borough* of Professor Maitland; from the *Cambridge Borough Charters*, edited by Miss Bateson, and introduced by Professor Maitland; from Miss Bateson's *Cambridge Gild Records*, with introduction by Dr Cunningham; and from the *Liber Memorandorum Ecclesie de Bernewelle*, edited by Mr J. W. Clark. I should be ungrateful indeed if I did not

v

add that the Publications and Communications of the Cambridge Antiquarian Society have supplied me with invaluable materials for reconstituting Cambridge in the remoter and more immediate past. Among many whose contributions I have found helpful I would mention particularly Professor Hughes, Sir W. Hope, Mr J. E. Foster, Dr Stokes and Dr Palmer. But the list is as interminable as my debt to them and others is immeasurable. One complaint I have to make—that the Society has issued no General Index of its recent issues; my paper-bound copies have been reduced to rags.

Two criticisms I anticipate and would disarm. In much that I have written I have disregarded chronological sequence, and have preferred to trace the growth of conditions and institutions in continuous process. The plan has led to some repetitions, but I think that it will best explain how Cambridge from what it was has come to be what it is. Also I have not dwelt at any length on the annals of the town since 1835. For the events of that time I would refer the reader to directories and guide-books. Those events may be the history of to-morrow. I cannot judge of their importance, and I am not greatly interested in the conscious and organised 'movements' of modern times. I am not prepared to say which seed will grow and which will not. There never was an age that did not think that in it was summed the wisdom of all past time, and I know not that the present age differs therein from those that went before it. The gropings and blunderings of our barbarous sires are far more interesting; and they make a *History*.

For permission to reproduce pictures which are their copyright or in their possession my best thanks are due to the Syndics of the Cambridge University Press and the University Library: also to the Editor, *Cambridge Daily News*, to Mr A. B. Gray, author of *Cambridge Revisited :* to Mr W. A. Fenton, Borough Librarian, to Lt.-Col. B. W. Beales and to Mrs F. S. Macaulay : to Messrs Scott and Wilkinson who are responsible for the photographic reproductions: and lastly to Mr E. W. Heffer, who has spared no pains in producing the book, in respect of form, type and illustration, in a manner which is highly creditable to the publishing firm of which he is a managing director.

ARTHUR GRAY.

October, 1925.

Contents

List of Illustrations

PAGE

CHAPTER I.

The Roman Town

In the year 673 Aethelthryth (Etheldreda), daughter of Anna, King of the East Angles, ' began the minster at Ely,' as the Anglo-Saxon Chronicle tells us; and there she lived as abbess until her death, seven years later. What followed may be told in the words of Bede, whose Ecclesiastical History was written within forty years of the event recorded.

'Etheldreda was succeeded in the office of abbess by her sister Sexburga, who had been married to Earconberct, King of Kent. When Etheldreda had been buried sixteen years the same abbess resolved to raise her bones, place them in a new coffin and remove them to the church. She ordered some of the brethren to look for a stone wherewith to make a coffin with this object. They took ship—as the district of Ely is entirely surrounded with waters and fens, and has no large stones—and came to a certain desolate little city, situated not far away, which in the English language is called Grantacaestir. And presently they found near the walls of the city a coffin beautifully fashioned of white marble, closely fitted with a lid of the same material. So, perceiving that the Lord had prospered their journey, they gave thanks and brought it with them to the monastery.'[1]

What and where was this desolate little city? Roman unquestionably. Bede's word is *civitatula*, a diminutive of *civitas*, and *civitas* in his Latin always means a Roman settlement. As much is implied by the termination—*caestir*, which is Northumbrian for the West Saxon *ceaster*, Latin *castra*, words which survive in the *-chester* or *-caster* of so many English place-names. There are two villages by the river Granta, or Cam, and close to Cambridge whose present names contain the *chester* element—Chesterton and Grantchester.

Naturally some antiquarians have identified Granta-caestir with the latter; and apparently not without

---

[1] *Eccl. Hist.* iv. 19.

reason. The place, if not desolate, is little enough to this day to fit Bede's description. Moreover there is some sort of earthwork there which might conceivably be Roman, and there are a few Roman tiles embedded in the church walls; as Smith, the weaver, said of the handicraft of Jack Cade's father, 'the bricks are alive at this day to testify it.' Roman remains, however, are plentiful on every side of Cambridge—so plentiful indeed that Dr Caius, the sixteenth century historian of Cambridge University, constructed out of them an imaginary Roman city stretching over the two miles which separate Grantchester from the Castle Hill. But, we may ask, is it likely that the Ely brethren, having brought their 'ship' up a fairly broad and easily navigable river as far as Chesterton, passed by the conspicuous Roman chester which looked down on the river there, and poled or towed the ship up the narrow, winding course of the upper river to a site so insignificant as Grantchester has always been? The supposed walls of Grantchester fall flat as those of Jericho, when we discover that the name of the place is a relatively modern corruption of the medieval Grantsete, *i.e.*, settlers by the river Granta.

So to Chesterton we turn to seek this desolate little city. And in the village which clusters about Chesterton church we shall not find it. 'No traces of Roman work have been noticed at Chesterton,' writes Professor C. C. Babington in his *Ancient Cambridgeshire*. But the Professor did not reckon with a singular circumstance. The great mound and quadrangular ramparts of earth which we still call Cambridge Castle, though of castellated buildings no trace remains, stands in what we may justly consider the oldest part of Cambridge. Singularly enough it is not and, for as many ages as we can trace backwards, never has been a part of Cambridge town, but has always been included in Chesterton parish. The anomaly may be feudal and artificial. But so much is certain; Chesterton takes its name from the chester, and in days, it may be, before Cambridge town existed or had a name, the chester was in Chesterton township.

There can be no manner of doubt that the coffin-stone which the Ely brethren carried off was brought from near the Castle Hill, and with some certainty we may fix rather precisely where they found it. About the year 890 Bede's History was translated by King Alfred, or under his direction, into the West Saxon variety of the Anglo-Saxon speech. In one version of the translation it is stated that the brethren found the stone ' by the stream walls of Granta.' About the middle of the twelfth century a certain monk of Ely, Thomas by name, retold Bede's story in a Latin book called *Historia Eliensis*, and he adds the observation that the stone was found ' in a place which to the present day is called Armeswerch.'[1] From a medieval source of information we know that Armeswerch was situated between the river and the high bank in Magdalene College grounds, which probably is in the position of the southern face of the *vallum*, or rampart, of the Roman stronghold.[2]

The desolation of this little city, or ' ruined chester,' as Alfred translates Bede's words, throws a vivid gleam of light on the conditions of Britain after the withdrawal of the Roman legions in 411. It seems incredible that a site so important as Cambridge, whether as a military stronghold or as a centre of trade, should have remained uninhabited for close on three centuries. Yet for a much longer period such was the condition of a station more important than Cambridge—Castra Legionum, the Anglo-Saxon Legeceastre, modern Chester, which, as late as in the year 894, is described in the Anglo-Saxon Chronicle as a ' waste chester.' Silchester, York, probably even London, stood utterly untenanted for a period, longer or shorter, after the Anglo-Saxon inroads. The English invaders, like

[1] *Hist. Eliensis* i. 26. [2] *Liber Memorandorum* iii. 97.

their Teutonic forefathers of whom Tacitus writes, regarded walled towns as strongholds of slavery. Superstition was a motive for their avoidance not less strong than the passion for liberty. Many a Roman site was looked on as the haunt of supernatural and malevolent powers. A Saxon *scop*, or gleeman, sang,

> Chesters are seen afar
> Skilled work of giants that are on the earth,

and the same description of 'giants' work' is given by an earlier bard to the cavern inhabited by the monstrous Grendel.

In Cambridge—at least in a part of it—there is evidence that for long ages the site was given over to solitude. The Roman camp was of course designed to guard the passage of the river where it was crossed by the road which is now represented by Bridge Street and Magdalene Street. The ground here on either bank was low and swampy. In medieval times part of St Clement's parish was known as the Holm, a name given to land liable to floods. Between the river and the present road-crossing opposite St Sepulchre's Church Roman engineers constructed on the peaty surface a solid causeway of squared beams of wood laid upon piles driven into the soil. In the year 1823 this causeway was discovered in a good state of preservation. It was fourteen feet beneath the present level of the street, and as there were several feet of peat above it, it is evident that it had been long disused and forgotten when this ancient part of Cambridge was built.[1]

About this Roman camp, or town, local historians have assumed as proven much which better knowledge confesses to be based on scanty evidence. What is known is almost entirely negative. The mount on

---

[1] Babington, *Ancient Cambridgeshire*, 26, 27 (C.A.S. 8vo. Publ.). In times comparatively recent the river channel near the Great Bridge was artificially narrowed. In excavating for the foundation of Messrs. Cox's garage on the Quay Side some upright posts were found. They were scored with the marks of ropes by which barges had been tethered to the river bank.

the river side of the Castle bailey is not a Roman work; almost certainly, like similar mounts in other castles, it was raised after the Conquest, probably by the Conqueror in 1068. Likewise the high banks seen in Magdalene College grounds, near Storey's almshouses and facing New Chesterton, are in the main of the same date, though in parts they have been heightened in more recent times. It is likely enough that they have been built over the *vallum* of the Roman camp.[1] But with respect to the position of the Praetorium and the Decuman and other gates on which imaginative archaeologists of former times claimed such precise knowledge it is wise to share the scepticism of Edie Ochiltree about 'Praetorian here, Praetorian there,' until ocular evidence has convinced us of the 'bigging' of them.

One point of interest arises out of Bede's story. His city had walls (*muros*), which an ordinary camp had not. That Bede means walls of masonry and not earthen mounds is clear from another passage in his History where he writes: 'a wall (*murus*) is made with stones, but a rampart (*vallum*), with which camps are fortified to repel the attacks of enemies, is made of sods cut out of the ground.' Grantacaestir then belonged to the class of towns such as York, Silchester and Colchester, which, owing their origin to military camps, developed into permanent centres of population and commerce. Bowtell, the Cambridge antiquarian of a century ago, records that in 1804 portions of walls of Roman brick were unearthed near the turnpike gate on the Huntingdon road and also in the eastern and western sides of the camp. Roman remains of all sorts may be found in and near the Castle area, but of Roman walls there I know no evidence except Bowtell's.[2]

[1] St. John Hope, *The Norman Origin of Cambridge Castle* in C.A.S. *Comm.* xi. 324.

[2] C.A.S. *Comm.* viii. 189.

CHAPTER II.

The Site

IN a momentary parting of the cloud which envelops English History in the ages succeeding the Roman occupation we have seen, in the last years of the seventh century, a deserted site, broken walls, and outside them the tombs of a forgotten people; and the name of the place, we are told, was Grantacaestir. Two silent centuries pass, and on this same site we see something that may be called a town, a town of so much importance that it has a bridge, and therefore calls itself Grantebrig. The empty chester with its haunting giants has dissolved itself out of the foreground; in its place we see upon the bridge hordes of freebooting Danes. They 'sat' at Grantebrig for a whole year in 875.

There is history and there is romance in place-names. In the ages before the coming of the English invaders Grantacaestir was apparently known to the Briton as Caer-grant. How the Roman called it we do not know; for its traditional identification with Camboritum, a place mentioned in the Itinerary of Antoninus, rests on little more than an illusory resemblance to the name Cambridge, which is a relatively modern corruption of the medieval name of the town, Cantebrig; and even Cantebrig yields in antiquity to Grantebrig, which was always the name in use from the end of the ninth to the middle of the twelfth century.[1]

In Grantebrig the first element is Grant, or Granta, which, as Alfred's translation of Bede tells us, was the name of the river at Cambridge—a name not Saxon, but probably Celtic. In later times we sometimes

---

[1] Skeat, *Place-Names of Cambridgeshire*, 29–32 (C.A.S. 8vo. Publ.).

find the river called the Ree, or Rhee (compare river-names such as Rhe-nus, Rye), or the Ee, which is simply Anglo-Saxon for 'water.' It was not till a much later age that it came to be called Cant (compare Kent, Kennett), and Cam is a form of the name not earlier than 1600.

The second element *brycg*, or *brig*, is interesting. It refers to the bridge near Magdalene College, which in later times was magniloquently called the Great Bridge. As a monument of engineering skill the present bridge is neither great nor beautiful. But of its Bridge Cambridge once made particular and reasonable boast. It is represented in the first Seal of the Borough, executed in 1423, and the townsmen made special glory of it in their address to James I when he visited the town in 1615. It is noteworthy that Cambridge is the only parliamentary borough, Cambridgeshire the only county, in England whose name contains the *bridge* element. All other names in which it occurs are of unimportant places situated on insignificant streams. The first appearance in written English of the word *bridge*, which in one form or another is common to all Teutonic languages, is in the name Grantebrycge in the Anglo-Saxon Chronicle (in the year 875); and there is the best reason to believe that the bridge at Cambridge—no doubt a wooden structure—was the first of any consequence erected in England since the departure of the Romans.

Why did men first congregate at Cambridge, or why, for that matter, did any primitive English town grow up on this site rather than on that? A minefield or a convenient haven in more recent times may foster centres such as Middlesbrough or Cardiff; but the Saxons knew no mines, and the danger of pirate raids induced them to prefer inland situations for their dwellings. After the Conquest a castle, a cathedral or a monastery would draw to itself a population of trading civilians; but castles and cathedrals were not of

Saxon times, and monasteries were too poor and unimportant to give employment to merchants and artisans. A situation on a navigable and preferentially a tidal river was ideal for trading purposes. Conditions complementary and essential were that the site should be well above the river level and not subject to floods, that there should be good road communications and a river passage by ford or bridge.

The first settlements within the borough area were undoubtedly on its ' hills ' : the Castle Hill on one side of the river, and on the other Market Hill, Peas Hill, St. Andrew's Hill—once veritable eminences above the marsh. Along the river banks from the Great Bridge to the mill-pool above Queens' College were low grounds unfitted for permanent habitation. Dwelling houses were not built there until after times when the surface was artificially raised.

Primitive Cambridge was well provided with land communications. The roads made by the Romans, as Bede testifies, were still in use in his day and for long centuries afterwards served as the great arteries of commerce. On the north-western side of the Roman station two such Ways intersected. The one of them, known in very early times as Akeman Street, followed the open downs of chalk which reach from the Norfolk coast to the upper waters of the Thames, and thence to the English Channel : of it we shall have to say something presently. The other road, to which antiquarians have given the name Via Devana, starting from Colchester, entered Cambridgeshire near Horseheath, whence as far as Red Cross on the Hills Road it exists in the grass-way marked in maps as Worsted Street, but anciently called Wolf Street Way. Through Cambridge it is continued in the main street leading from the neighbourhood of the Railway Station to the Castle, and thence goes on to Godmanchester and Leicester: it may have been prolonged, though it is not certain, as far as to Deva (Chester), from which it derives its name. At Godmanchester it joined the Ermine Street, which went from London through Lincoln to the Humber.

It is a noteworthy circumstance that between London and Cambridge there was no direct route in Roman and Saxon times. There is no 'London Road' at Cambridge. London has an Oxford Street, but it has no highway called Cambridge Street. The direct southern route between Cambridge and London was practically barred by the steep edge of the East Anglian Heights between Saffron Walden and Baldock, and by the tangled woods and heavy clay of Hertfordshire beyond them; and the forest of Essex was a like obstacle on the eastern side. If the East Anglian of Cambridge would travel to London by the highway his route was extremely devious. He must strike the old British track called Icknield Way at Royston, and go by it as far west as Dunstable, where it met the Ermine Street, and thence, turning east again, he passed through St Albans. The difficulty of the route had a notable effect on the character and destinies of early Cambridge. For purposes of trade London was a foreign town. To its kings Cambridge owed no fealty. The pulsations of its life did not circulate to Cambridge—scarcely reached it until far down in the Middle Ages. Along great highways and over open downs a Danish host, horsing themselves in East Anglia, raced repeatedly through Cambridge, to York, to Wareham, to Thetford: they never tried to force their way to London. So it remained in later times. King John descends on the Marshland from Lincoln, and the barons reach Cambridge from Windsor.

As the Danish raids proved, it was by no means an unmixed advantage to Cambridge that it lay at the junction of two highways. Conditions must have been much the same in the long ages of tribal fighting which succeeded the English invasion of the fifth century. The East Anglian farmer who would secure

B

his homestead from burning and pillaging hordes did not plant it on one of the great high roads; to this day the Roman routes from Cambridge are almost bare of habitation. Consequently this gathering of houses near the Cambridge cross-roads points to a day like that of Jael, when the highways were no longer unoccupied, nor were travellers forced to walk in byways. With peace came river traffic, to which, as much as to its roads, primitive Cambridge owed its being and prosperity. The tidal waters waxed as far as Waterbeach, and as far as Cambridge the channel was deep enough to carry sea-going vessels. Except at Ely, whose practically insular position in the Fens debarred it from landward trade, there was no extent of high ground about the river until Cambridge was reached.

In strictness Grantabrycge is a locative case, and the meaning is 'at Granta bridge,' which may imply that the bridge was built before the houses. If the Romans had made a bridge it is evident that it had ceased to exist in 696, and between that year and 875 we must place the erection of the Saxon bridge. It is not unlikely that it was the work of Offa, king of the Mercians from 758 to 796. He was a great builder, and created the two monasteries of Bath and St Albans. He encouraged trade and negotiated with Charlemagne a treaty for the protection and taxation of merchants passing beyond sea. For a season the inter-tribal wars which for two centuries had wasted Mercia and East Anglia ceased when he reduced the latter to his over-lordship. He had motives both military and commercial for making an easy access from inland Mercia to the eastern coast, and the obvious route lay through Cambridge.

In the meagre chronicle of events happening in Saxon Cambridge we hear nothing of a castle. Yet it is hard to believe that the Bridge was altogether unprotected by some kind of fortress, for which the old chester afforded a suitable site. Indeed that a *burh* was in existence in pre-Norman and probably pre-Danish times is evidenced by the fact that various properties in the county were charged with a tax for the maintenance and reparation of a *burh* at Cambridge. This tax was known as *burhbote*, in later times as ' castle-ward.' Castles of stone were unknown in England until Norman days, and, no doubt, the Cambridge *burh* was a timbered structure of the pattern of the many *burhs* set up after 913 as a defence against the Danes. No vestige of it remains at the present day.[1]

---

[1] In 1810 seven more or less complete gravestones with ornament of an 'Anglo-Saxon' (?Danish) pattern were discovered on the S.E. side of the old Gate-house of the Castle. Clearly they had originally stood above ground, but had been buried, from four to six feet deep, under the Norman rampart of the bailey. It may be conjectured that before the Conquest the mother church of Cambridge stood within this Roman camp; if so, it was no doubt a timber structure, destroyed perhaps when the Danes burnt the town in 1010, perhaps when the site was cleared for the building of the Castle. There are abundant examples of churches built within British earthworks or Roman camps; the choice of site was dictated either by considerations of superstitious conservatism or of defence. There is at Ickleton, Cambs., a place known as 'Sunken Church,' which is known to be the site of a Roman 'basilica.' It should be observed that the stone chosen for the entombment of Etheldreda was unmistakably of Roman workmanship; no stone *coffins* of Saxon type have been found in the Castle area.

CHAPTER III.

The Saxon Town

By the so-called Treaty of Wedmore (878) Cambridge-shire, along with East Anglia and half Mercia, passed under the rule of Danish kings and became subject to Danish law; and so it remained until the middle of the following century. One relic of Danish rule survived at Cambridge when the Domesday Survey was made—a class of 'lawmen' (*lagemanni*), such as existed at Lincoln and Stamford. The existence of this class, perhaps corresponding to the 'bailiffs' of later times, may indicate that Grantebrig had reached a semi-corporate stage, distinguishing it from the rural vills of the shire. Otherwise there is little to remind us of the Danish occupation of the town and shire. In the eleventh century the population of the shire seems to have been almost exclusively English: in Domesday hardly a Danish name is to be found among the tenants of the soil. In the village names there is hardly a trace of Danish settlements. The termination *-by*, characteristic of them, is wholly absent from Cambridge-shire, though it is common in the Mercian shires, and not unknown in Norfolk and Suffolk. More than that—the fact that Cambridgeshire place-names contain no element such as *church* or *minster* or Saints' names is evidence that the district was fully settled before Augustine brought Christianity to Britain in 597.

But one important result followed from the Danish conquest. The Danes divided the parts of England subject to them into shires, naming each after some town contained in it which was in some sort regarded as a county town. In the ninth century, as now, the only considerable town in the shire was Cambridge. Wisbech and Ely, both the property of the Abbot of Ely, were not recognised as boroughs in the Domesday Survey. The importance of Cambridge is shown by the fact that it was reckoned as a hundred independent of the sixteen hundreds into which rural Cambridge was divided.

The annals of Cambridge begin with its occupation by the Danes in 875. From thence for some centuries onwards the tale that they tell is meagre, disjointed and colourless. It is to other sources that we must look if we would invest the bare bones of chronicle with life and breath. We shall find them in incidents of law and custom, in topography and the evidence of place-names, in the discoveries of archaeology, and in the suggestions which documents of the later middle ages supply. In their light the history of the origin of Cambridge town becomes of unique interest. Details fall into their place, and hypothesis takes on itself the aspect of certainty. We must endeavour to fit the history of the town into the general history of England, and particularly of the district to which it belongs.

One of the most striking features in the geological structure of Britain is the long band of chalk which reaches from the north coast of Norfolk to the south coast of Devon. Roman engineers recognised the military advantages offered by this tract of land, unencumbered by forest or fen, for the construction of a great highway—the Akeman Street mentioned in the last chapter. Nature herself dictated to the rude tribes who preceded the Romans the same route. Running roughly parallel with the Akeman Street, on its S.E. side, is the older thoroughfare known as the Icknield Way. From Thetford, in Norfolk, it went by Newmarket to Chesterford, where it crossed the upper waters of the Cam, and so on by Royston to Streatley on the Thames. The Isle of Ely is the alluvial deposit of the Fenland rivers. The westward limit of the chalk in Cambridgeshire is the river Cam in its course between Waterbeach, below Cambridge, and its source at Ashwell. Beyond the Cam the surface formation is gault. Cambridge is exactly at the extremity of chalk and gault.

Akeman Street ended on the coast at Holme, near Hunstanton, where King Edmund the Martyr, coming from Old Saxony, in modern Sleswig, disembarked. Near this the open coast was defended by the Roman camp at Branodunum, or Brancaster. The road ran by way of Castle Acre, Denver, Ely, then through a tract of fen to Landbeach, where the gault begins, and so to the Castle at Cambridge.

In connection with these two roads the names of the villages which border them have a remarkable tale to tell. I have already commented on the primitive character of Cambridgeshire place-names: we may assume that the English occupation of the shire was completed in the course of the sixth century. The country has few outstanding natural features, and there is a consequent monotony in the type of village names. About half of them end in -*ham* or -*ton*, either termination betokening the homestead of the original settler or family.

Here we are confronted with a curious phenomenon. Villages with the *ham* ending are thickly grouped all over the chalk country from Brancaster in one direction to Chesterford in another: *tons* are almost completely absent. Between Akeman Street and the Wash and as far as Denver there is a strip of gault; there, as if by magic, the *tons* appear. As far as the edge of the fen between Stretham and Landbeach the *hams* continue to line the Akeman Street. The ancient name of Landbeach was Beche, significantly marking the low brink of the southern edge of the fen. Beyond the fen the gault begins again: the two *tons* of Milton and Chesterton at once remind us of the change of surface. Teversham marks the approximate limit of the chalk next Cambridge. Eastward of the Street the country of the *hams* extends as far as Thetford and Bury, beyond which the soil changes and *hams* and *tons* are intermixed. The *hams* die out near the Essex border, where London clay begins.

On the western side of the Cam, where the soil is gault or greensand, *tons* are as predominant as *hams* in the region just described, and they extend into the bordering shires of Bedford, Huntingdon and North-ampton, where *hams* are all but unknown. Beginning at Barton the *tons* line the whole length of Akeman Street to the S.W. border of the county. Hereabouts the *tons* stray over the Bedfordshire border into the chalk land.

Ham and *ton* being identical in meaning the only explanation of this remarkable distribution of the two terminations must be that they mark the settlements of distinct tribes, or, which may be the same thing, that one of them is older than the other. We may safely conclude that *ham* is the more primitive. It was the word which the English brought with them from their continental home; *ton* in any form is virtually unknown there. In our numerous Hamptons it is evident that the suffixed *ton* has been added to an original *ham* when the latter had gone out of use as the mark of a settlement. And this conclusion accords with the undoubted fact that in the invasions of the English the open country was first occupied. If the duality of the origin of the Cambridgeshire folk be conceded there can be no doubt which were the people who settled in either district. The men of the chalk downs were East Anglians, those of the gault were Mercians. And we may fairly infer that the former were the first comers, at least in Cambridgeshire.

Both these peoples were of Anglian origin, and came from the district in Sleswig called Angel; and they spoke a nearly identical language. History has nothing to tell us of their first coming. Their first emergence is about the beginning of the seventh century, when Raedwald, king of the East Anglians, was recognised as Bretwalda, and was the most powerful of the tribal kings. In 637 Penda, the Mercian king, ravaged the whole of East Anglia and slew in succession three East Anglian kings; but on his death in 655 East Anglia recovered its independence. It was again subjugated by Offa, who was king of Mercia from 758 to 796. Kite and crow warfare continued between the two races until 827, when both kingdoms were subjected to Wessex. After the Danish occupation they were completely fused.

Contemporary history is silent about the boundaries of these kingdoms. But William of Malmesbury tells us that East Anglian kings ruled in the shire of Grantebrige, and that Ely was included in their dominion; and from other sources we learn the significant fact that, before the erection of a see at Ely, the monks of Ely always refused recognition of the Mercian bishop of Dorchester (Oxfordshire), and claimed attachment to the East Anglian see of Thetford or Elmham. On the other hand the curious circumstance that Cambridgeshire has always shared with Huntingdonshire its county officer, the sheriff, seems to imply that the former shire was in some sort reckoned as part of Mercia. The sheriff was, in theory, the deputy of the earl, and at the time of the Conquest Waltheof, as earl of Huntingdon, claimed, as part of the Honour of Huntingdon, a large number of manors in Cambridgeshire. All of them lay in the south-western portion of the shire, where *tons* predominate. We may therefore conclude that these parts were regarded as belonging to the Mercian earldom of Huntingdon. Other inferences pointing to the same conclusion may be drawn from the Hundred Rolls Survey made in the reign of Edward I. A variety of estates in the Mercian parts of the shire were then charged with the ancient payments of *burhbote* and *brycg-geweorc*, the former for the maintenance of the Castle, the latter for the repair of the Bridge at Cambridge. As no East Anglian estate was burdened with these charges we must infer that they were imposed at a time when the Castle and the Bridge were both in the hands of the Mercians.

Cambridge town stands at the verge of the chalk region, and both *ham* and *ton* appear in the names of neighbouring villages: at one end of the town is Chesterton, at the other Newnham. To which of the two peoples did it belong? Or was the site, perchance, settled by both?

In the metrical chronicle called *Lestorie des Engles* written in Norman-French by Gaimar, it is said: 'The city of Grancestre once belonged to Mercia, and ought to do so; one king could well protect it if he could hold it in peace.' Gaimar wrote about the year 1140, but the fact that he uses the old name of the town, Grancestre, would indicate that he used some much older source of information. His words seem to imply that the possession of the town by the Mercian kings was disputed by kings of another race. They must have been East Anglian. From other sources we are led to the conclusion that at an early period the town was shared by the two peoples, or rather, that there were two towns, the northern in the hands of the Mercians, the southern occupied by East Anglians.

In times indefinitely remote and down to recent days every English village was encompassed by a wide tract of land containing innumerable strips, resembling allotments, which were cultivated by the inhabitants of the village. This tract was called distinctively the Field, and was usually divided into three parts, also called fields, which were cultivated in turn in three successive seasons of grain, etch and fallow. As no township was without its Field, so none had more than one Field in the collective sense. The curious feature about Cambridge is that it had two, each an agricultural unit cultivated on the three-field system. The Field on the northern and western sides of the town was called Cambridge Field; that on the southern and eastern sides was generally known as Barnwell Field. Each Field contained about 1200 acres, or about ten hides, which was about the size of a village Field.[1] In the later middle ages each strip was charged with payment of tithe to some parish church. It is significant that, with very few exceptions, the strips in Cambridge Field were tithed to the churches in the northern and transpontine quarter of town and to St Clement's, next the Bridge, and those in Barnwell Field to the churches in the southern parts. The duplicate Field seems to have its origin in a twofold community, and in a time when each part of the town was reckoned as an ecclesiastical unit possessed of its church. The recognition of the obligation to pay tithe dates from the eighth century: the field system goes back to a much earlier date.

Another singular fact is presented to us by Dr Caius in his History of the University, written in the sixteenth century. In his day there existed on the north side of the Castle a cross of stone called the Market Cross, and there was then a tradition that the Market of the old town was held about it. There is evidence going back to the thirteenth century of the existence of the market in the place where it is still held, but the Borough records contain no hint of a market beyond the river. If it existed it must have been in a very early period, and if the two markets existed contemporaneously such a phenomenon can only be explained by the hypothesis that there were two independent trading communities.

[1] Each of the two Fields had its own pound for the restraint of straying cattle. That of Cambridge Field, which existed until the beginning of the present century, was on the southern side of what is still called Pound Hill. The other, which is marked in Loggan's plan of 1688, stood in the middle of the present Fair Street, opposite Midsummer Common.

St. Benet's Church in 1842

If we consider the nature of the soil on which Cambridge has grown we shall more readily understand the curious juxtaposition of two townships independent and, as it would seem, occupied by hostile peoples. It is easy to understand that the slope rising from the river to the Castle would be peopled at a very early date. Of the southern town a large part, even in later middle ages, was water-logged and quite unfitted for permanent habitation. The first settlement must have been on the gravel terrace extending from Barnwell and the Botanic Garden to the low alluvial ground near St John's College and the Round Church. On this terrace was the Market Place and the oldest church in Cambridge, St Benet's.[1] Near the river was an expanse of alluvium, which, if not actually marsh, was liable to inundation. In process of ages the parts of the alluvium nearest the centre of the town were artificially heightened, and on the made ground rose the buildings of the earlier colleges and one parish church, St John's in Milne Street. But all through the Middle Ages the only erections on the river bank between the Great Bridge and the Mills were hithes. Similarly the grounds on the western side of the river, where the college grounds at the Backs are, was an unrelieved morass, traversed by a multiplicity of river-courses, which in recent centuries have been straightened into moats bounding the college grounds. This morass was an effective barrier between the two towns and the hostile races which occupied them.

The earliest extension on the southern bank of the river must have been in the neighbourhood of the Bridge. In the eleventh century one of the wards into which the town was divided was called ' brugge

---

[1] The tower of St. Benet's Church was probably built in the eleventh century, at a time when the memory of Danish incursions was recent. Like other Saxon towers in the eastern parts of England, its structure indicates that its purpose was as much defensive as ecclesiastical. Originally it had no external openings except in the highest of its three stages, and the windows in that stage could only be reached from outside by ladders. It is recorded that in 1010, when the Danes were ravaging Cambridgeshire, a brave man at Balsham defended himself against a host of the marauders, standing on a step of the church tower.

ward,' and it contained thirty-two dwellings—about the average number which made up a ward. It is to be remarked that the area of St Clement's parish seems to have been reckoned as part of the northern town; for the church drew its tithes from Cambridge Field. At first sight this looks like an arbitrary arrangement: a consideration of the conditions of primitive Cambridge shows it to be natural and what might be expected. It is a constant rule that where an important road crossed a river which was a tribal boundary the ford or bridge must be exclusively in the possession of one of the two peoples. In this case the passage, whether by bridge or ford, appears to have been controlled by the Mercians. At the Small Bridges, which crossed branches of the river between Silver Street and Newnham, the East Anglians seem to have held both banks, since at that point and nowhere else one of the southern parishes extends across the old river channels. A deep ditch, beginning from the river at St John's College Library and rejoining it near the Electric Works, parted St Clement's parish from the southern town.

Except in the Bridge quarter the two towns were parted by the river Cam and by the swamps which bordered it. The extinction of the old hostility and the obliteration of the tribal boundary was the outcome of the Danish conquest. It is typical of the unification of England which was the unlooked-for result of that event.[1]

---

[1] In this chapter I have summarized the evidence collected in my *Dual Origin of the Town of Cambridge* (C.A.S. 4to Publ. New Series, No. I.) and *The Ford and Bridge of Cambridge* (C.A.S. *Comm.* xiv. 126–139).

CHAPTER IV.

Domesday Cambridge

DR CAIUS, writing in his History of the University (1574), places an 'eversion' of Cambridge by the Danes in or about the year 870, and local historians, and even Freeman, have repeated his assertion. I know no contemporary record of the event, though it is certain that another generation of Danes did burn the town in 1010. Between these dates Cambridge seems to have been in a thriving way. Clearly it was held to be the shire town. It ranked as a complete hundred, independent of the county. Norwich and Thetford held the same rank in Norfolk; but Ipswich and Bedford were only half-hundreds, and Huntingdon no more than a quarter-hundred. In the tenth and eleventh centuries there was a royal mint at Cambridge. Disputed cases at law were referred to hundred meetings held there. One such meeting is recorded as taking place at the Bridge, another 'under Thernigefeld, near Maidenburg,' which we may conjecture was in the neighbourhood of the Castle.[1] Ely monks acquire farm lands within the borough. Trade prospers and merchants arrive from Ireland in ships to sell 'wares and cloaks' to the burgesses.[2] There is a gild of thegns at Grantabrycge—seemingly country gentlemen who meet there. The rules which it drew up show that it was a kind of mutual insurance and benefit society, with much the same fines and forfeits for breach of regulations that a modern club of the kind exacts. There is a lord, or president (*comes*) of the gild, and reeves or country justices are members;

---

[1] *Liber Eliensis* ii. 135, 137.　　[2] *Ibid.* ii. 148.

among higher dignitaries there is mention of an alderman. Fines are paid in cash or in ' systers ' (*sextarii*) of honey. Incidentally we learn that some ' churls' are Welshmen (*i.e.* British by descent), and that a Welsh churl's person is reckoned at half the value of an English churl's. Provision is made for the sickness and death of members, and at the funeral feast of a member it is appointed that his fellows shall offer alms at St Etheldreda's altar at Ely, apparently as being the religious centre of the shire.

Of the ' sitting ' of the Danes at Cambridge in the two centuries following 870 there is not much to be said. They instituted a ruling caste of ' lawmen,' of which I shall presently have something to remark. To their sea-faring activity may be attributed the commercial consequence of the town in pre-Conquest times, and the ships which brought to it Irish wares were, no doubt, owned and manned by Danish settlers at Dublin and Wexford. They seem to have established themselves principally in the neighbourhood of the Bridge. In a list of Cambridge dwellers amerced to the King in 1177 is a certain Turketell of the Bridge, and in a similar list of 1211 is the significant name of Ketel the Merchant. Ketel and Thorketel are definitely Norse names. St Clement's church furnishes other evidence of their occupation of the quarter, Clement being a favourite Danish saint, as is testified by St Clement Danes in London. Part of St Clement's parish, adjoining the Bridge, was known in the early thirteenth century as the Holm (*hulmus*) : ' holm,' with the meaning ' low ground liable to flood,' is an exclusively Scandinavian word.

In 1068 it is said that the Conqueror, on his return from the subjugation of the North of England, built a Castle at Cambridge, and to make a site for it caused twenty-seven houses to be destroyed. Of this Castle no vestige remains. Probably it was a hasty erection of no great size or solidity, for in the following year it was occupied by the King during his assault on the Camp of Refuge in the Isle of Ely. The expression used by the Barnwell chronicler that King Edward I 'began' the Castle in 1283 would imply that its Norman predecessor had either disappeared or was removed in that year.[1]

William's great Survey of England, described in Domesday Book, was completed about the year 1086. The Ely chronicler—an Englishman with an Englishman's detestation of foreign despotism—describes the inquisition. He says:

> 'The King laid on the English an intolerable tribute, and gave instructions for making a survey of the whole of England, stating the amount of land held by each of his own men, the number of subtenants, ploughs, villeins, stock, even the amount to the last farthing of hard money possessed by each man, and the income derived from every holding.'[2]

The object of the enquiry being simply fiscal, we shall not look in Domesday Book for much light on the social, religious and commercial conditions of eleventh century Cambridge. Such as it is, the picture it gives of the town, both at the date of the survey and on the day when King Edward the Confessor was 'alive and dead,' is of extraordinary interest and value. To a certain extent the information which it gives is supplemented by the contemporaneous evidence of the Inquisition of the County of Cambridge, which is the original return from which Domesday Book was compiled, and of the Inquisitio Eliensis, a survey of land belonging to Ely monastery. From these sources we learn the following facts:

The borough of Grentebrige is a hundred in itself: that is to say it pays geld to the King as for a hundred hides of land—fully five times as much as an average

---

[1] In 1156 the sheriff, Pain Peverell, charges the Exchequer with the small sum of 7s. 7½d. for 'work' at the Castle. He charges a larger sum, £7, for work at the King's Hall, wherein he doubtless resided. This Hall is probably to be identified with 'the Sale,' which was the name given in later middle ages to a piece of ground on the north side of the Castle. *Sale* is Middle English for 'hall,' A.S. *sael*. In 1173, when the barons were making trouble in the north, the sheriff spent £31 on repairs at the Castle.

[2] *Liber Eliensis* ii. 104.

rural township would pay. Even to-day the borough includes within its limits, especially on its north-western side, a good deal of ordinary country: its area, before its extension in 1912, was about five square miles, which is about the size of an average Cambridgeshire township. Before the Conquest the levy originally called Danegeld was two shillings on each hide of land. The Conqueror increased it to six. Consequently the borough quota should have been £30; but the receipts were reduced by the large number of 'waste' holdings and by immunities allowed to certain tenants of Norman lords.

The 'customs' of the town, after these deductions, bring in £7, and 'landgable' adds a rather larger sum. Exactly what was comprised in the 'customs' it is hard to say. When the town purchased its liberties from King John it paid an annual sum of about £62 to the royal exchequer. It would seem that two important sources of the King's revenue from the town are not included in the 'customs' of Domesday Book—market tolls and the profits of the hundred court. Of the latter two-thirds went to the King and one-third to the earl. It would seem that 'land-gable,' which, in strictness, was the payment for strips in the common Field, included 'hagable,' the tax on houses in the town. These very ancient payments remained constant in amount for many centuries. The total produced was always a trifle more than £7, and the charge on individual holdings never varied.[1] The word 'hagable' is formed from Anglo-Saxon *haga*, a fenced or enclosed space, and *gafol*, payment. When the townsmen purchased from King John the

---

[1] In 1086 'landgable' produced £7 3s. 6d. In 1483 'hagable' produced £7 3s. 9d., but in the returns of the latter year 'lands,' *i.e.* in the Fields, are included and bring in much larger sums than 'tenements' in the town, most of which pay no more than 2d. The large total of £62 odd at which the borough was rated in King John's day seems to point to a considerable increase of population or in the valuation of town property. But it should be borne in mind that 'customs' in the Domesday return plainly do not include heriots and the very considerable profits of the King's mill, which in the return are said to produce £9.

privilege of holding the borough ' in farm ' these rents of course passed into the town treasury. In the seventeenth century the meaning of ' hagable ' was so far forgotten that it was interpreted as ' an ancient tenement having of old time broad gates.'

In the Confessor's time the town contained four hundred *masurae*, or tenements—which may be taken as a round number adopted for fiscal purposes—of which twenty-seven were destroyed to make the Norman Castle. Among occupants the Survey takes no notice of villeins, serfs and such-like persons, nor does it tell us the number of burgesses. There were ten wards in the town—in later times only seven. In the first ward was the Castle, and in the same ward several Norman lords had acquired slices of land out of the King's demesne, for which the sub-tenants paid the King no rent. The second ward is called ' brugge ward ' in the Inquisitio Eliensis, and presumably comprised the district near St Clement's church. The same authority states that the fourth ward contained a church belonging to the monastery at Ely, which can hardly be other than St Andrew's the Great. The third ward therefore may be taken as including Barnwell and the quarter now included in All Saints' parish. The remaining six wards must have been near the Market and the Mills. Transpontine Cambridge contains only fifty-four tenements out of the total of four hundred, and even in the Confessor's reign was much the least populous part of the town ; and so it continued to be two centuries later when the town was surveyed by the commissioners of Edward I.

Like any other hundred in the shire, Cambridge was in the jurisdiction of the sheriff, who collected the geld and such other dues as were charged to landowners: indeed, as being King's land and therefore subject to special ' customs,' it was worse off than most of its country neighbours. By all accounts Picot, the sheriff at the time of the Survey, was a hard and grasping man. The Cambridge men, with memories of old days of comparative ease and a dawning sense of municipal independence, were outspoken in their resentment at the new exactions laid on them by the King's officer. By a new 'custom' they were required to give some days of personal labour on the sheriff's farm—probably at Chesterton, for it does not seem that the King or the sheriff had farm-land in Cambridge —and they had moreover to find carts for him and lend their plough teams nine times a year instead of three, as had been the use in the Confessor's time. The sheriff had built three mills, depriving the town thereby of pasture and destroying certain houses. The former sheriff had demanded of each of the lawmen a sum of twenty shillings, as heriot, when he entered on his tenancy. Picot increased the amount to £8, as well as a palfrey and arms for one knight.

The incidental mention of lawmen (*lagemanni*) is interesting and challenges surmise. Evidently they were men of consequence, and the extortionate demand of £8 from them as succession due marks them as men of wealth and inheritors of wealthy fathers. The name and the office is not Saxon English, but Danish. Lawmen were to be found at Chester, Lincoln, Stamford —all of them towns in the Danelaw. They seem generally to have been twelve in number, and in some cases at least the office was hereditary. The English equivalent for the name might be 'domesmen.' Now between 1155 and 1175—a whole generation before King John granted the town in freedom to the burgesses—there was a certain Prior of Barnwell named Hugh Domesman. He was a great benefactor of the Priory, to which he gave 140 acres of land in Cambridge Fields as well as many tenements in the town. This property he inherited from his father, Osbert Domesman, who must have been living not far from the time of Domesday survey.[1]   Many of the plots in Cambridge

[1] *Liber Memorandorum*, 65, 98.

BURGVM DE GRENTEBRIGE p uno HVNDRET
se defend T.R.E. In hoc burgo fuer 7 sunt
dece custodie. In prima custodia .L.iiii. ma
ge ex his .ii. sunt Waste. In hac pma custodia ha
bent com .v. burgenses nichil reddentes. Comes mori
tonensis de tra Iudichel habet .iii. masuras. 7 ibi sunt .iii.
burgenses q T.R.E. reddeb .v. sol. 7 .viii. den 7 i. obolu
nichil reddunt. Radulf de bans habet .iii. in burg.
nichil reddent. Rogzer hō epi Remigii .iii. burg.
redd. Erchenger habet .i. burg. nichil reddit.
hec eade una custodia p duab. coputabat T.R.E.
p castro sunt destructe .xxvii. dom.
Secda custodia fuer .xl viii. masure T.R.E. ex his
.x. sunt Waste. De his .xiii. masure nichil reddit.
q .xxii. reddit oms csuetudines. De his hz Alan
burg nil redd. 7 ix manent in tris anglos
tertia custodia T.R.E. fuer .xl i. masura. Ex his sunt
.x. Waste. relique .xxx. reddunt oms consuetudines.
Quarta custodia T.R.E. fuer .xl v. masure. Ex his
.iiii. sunt Waste. relidue .xxx. redd oms csuetud.
Quinta custodia T.R.E. fuer .L. masure. Una ex his
Waste. alie oms reddunt csuetudines suas.
Septima custodia T.R.E. fuer .xxvii. masure. Tres
neri hnt de his iii. masuras. s. nichil reddit.
Octaua custodia T.R.E. fuer .xx vii. masure. Ex his
ista pter una tenet. 7 nichil reddit. / sunt .iii. Waste.
Nona custodia T.R.E. fuer .xxxii. masure. De his
Decima custodia T.R.E. fuer .xx ix. masure. Ex
his sunt .vii. Waste. tam se defendut.
De consuetudinib huí uille .vii. lib pannu 7 de
landgable .vii. lib. 7 ii. oris. 7 duo den.
Burgenses T.R.E. accomodabant uicecomiti carrucas
ter in anno. modo noue uicib. exigunt.
nec aueras nec curr T.R.E. inueniebant que m fa
ciunt p consuetudine imposita. Reclamant autem sup
Picotu uicecomite. comune pastura sibi p eu ablata.
q Picot fecit ibi iii. molendina. q aufert pastura 7 plures
domos destruunt. 7 molend unum abbis de Ely 7 alterum
.... comitis. Ipsa molendina redd ix lib p annu.
..hariecta lateramanet habuit isde Picot .viii. lib.
unu palefridu 7 uni militis arma.
Turri Godric sone qdo fuit uicecomes habuit
aueram unius istas .xx. solid.

i. Wills rex.	xxvi. Ardum de Scalers.
ii. Eps Wintoniensis.	xxvii. hugo de Bernefes.
iii. Eps Lincoliensis.	xxviii. hugo de port.
iiii. Eps Rofensis.	xxviiii. Ibericus de uer.
v. Abbas de Ely.	xxx. Eustachi de humedune.
vi. Abbas de S Edmundo.	xxxi. Wido de Rembecure.
vii. Abb de Ramesy.	xxxii. Petrus de Valonges.
viii. Abb de Torni.	xxxiii. Picot de grantebrige.
viiii. Abb de Croiland.	xxxiiii. Aunulf fr ilgeri.
x. Abb S Wandregisili.	xxxv. Oger filius Waleranni.
xi. Abbatia de Cetriz.	xxxvi. Wills filius Ansculfi.
xii. Comes mortoniensis.	xxxvii. Wills de Cahingei.
xiii. Comes Rogerius.	xxxviii. Robtus fastori.
xiiii. Comes Alanus.	xxxviiii. David de argentom.
xv. Comes Eustachius.	xl. Duo carpentarii regis.
xvi. Canonici baiocenses.	xli. Iudita comitissa.
xvii. Alueri Oisfard.	xlii. Azelina uxor Rad tallebosc.
xviii. Wills de Warenna.	xliii. uxor Boselini de diue.
xviiii. Ricard fili Gisleb.	xliiii. Rchenger pistor.
xx. Obtus de Todeni.	
xxi. Obtus gernon.	
xxii. Oisfrid de maneule.	
xxiii. isleba de gand.	
xxiiii. isleba fili giraldi.	
xxv. udo dapifer.	

TERRA REGIS   In Stapleho hund

Haban maneriu regis e p .xx. hid 7 dim se
defd. Tra e .xiiii. caruce. Ibi sunt .xvi. uilli 7 xvi.
bord cu .xii. car. In dnio .ii. car. 7 iii. serui. 7 u mold
.xxiiii. sol. De piscar. iii. mill 7 d. anguill pñ
xiiii. car. pastura ad pecun uille. Ibi .vii. piscatores
reddentes regi psentation pisciu ter m anno scdm qd
possunt. In totis ualentiis redd p annu .xx v. lib arsas
7 pensatas. 7 xiii. lib 7 vii. sol. 7 iiii. den ad numeru
de alb denar. p frumento brasio. melle 7 aliis minutis
csuetudinib. T.R.E. reddeb .xx v. lib ad numeru

Fields have names which suggest a very remote antiquity. One, which was at the Castle End, was called 'tun-mannys aker.' The *túnman*, or 'town-man,' was evidently an official, though, after Mayors came into existence, there is no record of him. I imagine that he was the counterpart of the town-reeve (*túngerefa*) of London, whose business was to collect 'customs.'[1] Peradventure he was the same person whom King John in his first charter (1201) calls the *prepositus* of Cambridge and associates with the sheriff in matters concerning tolls and customs. In his second charter (1207) the King grants to the burgesses that 'they shall make of themselves a *prepositus*.' It may be that before this he had been appointed by the King's sheriff, but it looks as though the grant was only a confirmation of what the earlier charter calls 'the ancient law of the borough.' Altogether, it seems likely that in the twelfth century, Cambridge had something like a Mayor and Bailiffs.[2]

But the town is copyhold of the King. The titles of property in the town are registered in the Court Rolls, which are kept by the sheriff at the Castle, and thither the householder must go if he would maintain his rights in actions at law. Not least of the advantages granted by King John was that transfers of property in the town were made in the borough court and duly witnessed by the Mayor and Aldermen.

Ploughs, carts, day-work in the fields give Cambridge, as the King's inquisitors saw it, the aspect of a rural

---

[1] Kemble, *The Saxons in England*, ii. 339.

[2] *Liber Memorandorum*, 238. Professor Maitland writes (*Doomsday and Beyond*, 95), 'The suitors are the doomsmen of the court,' *i.e.* those who 'owe suit' to the county or borough court, are bound to attend it, and pronounce its 'doom,' or decision; but he admits that the evidence that they bore the title of doomsmen is slight. Even serfs may owe suit. But the application of 'doomsman' in the case of Osbert and Hugh as a quasi-hereditary surname seems to imply an exceptional and official dignity. In one instance mentioned by Maitland (*ibid.* 211, note) *lawman* seems to = *doomsman*. I suggest that in the borough court of Cambridge, of which the sheriff was the presiding officer, 'the suitors' were an aristocratic hereditary class. The heriot required of the Cambridge lawmen consisted, besides a money payment, of a palfrey and the arms of a *miles*, which proves that they were reckoned as thegns of whom knight's service was exacted.

hamlet. If it had a market, fairs, hithes or churches, more than one, it was not the surveyors' business to mention them : tradesmen and artisans, as such, being untaxable, do not come into their scheme. There are three French-born residents : the English are so much strangers in their own town that some burgesses are said to live ' in the lands of the English,' *i.e.* outside the borough. Clearly we see what Cambridge was *not*. As a mere superficies of land it is one, a hundred. As a collective body of men, masters of their own affairs, it is not one, scarcely a body at all. In the lawmen there is a faint foreshadowing of good things to come ; but Mayors and Aldermen, the chosen trustees of a community, are people that we shall not hear about for a century. The greater corporation, the Universitas Scholarium, must wait yet longer before it comes to birth.

Before we dismiss the subject of the Conqueror's Survey, it is well to mention that Chesterton then was, as most of it still is, no part of Cambridge. Cambridge is a ' burg,' and it reckons as a hundred independent of other hundreds in the shire. Chesterton is only a ' vill,' or manor, and it belongs to the rural hundred of Chesterton. Like Cambridge, it pays toll to the King's exchequer by the hands of the sheriff ; but burg and manor were from the first distinct. Domesday Book carefully refrains from saying that Cambridge is a part of ' the King's land,' though it makes no question that Chesterton is royal demesne. From Cambridge the King receives hagable rent from houses, and ' customs,' no doubt, bring him more from tolls and market dues. Chesterton is a large manor, containing 30 hides, say 3600 acres, and it is rated highly in the King's book ; but its payment is the substitute for a payment in kind of corn, honey and malt, which marks it as purely rural. About the same date as his Cambridge charter King John (1200) divested himself of his Chesterton demesne, granting

it in perpetuity to the Prior and Canons of Barnwell
for an annual payment of £30 sterling. Thenceforth
it was ruled by the Prior's bailiff—an arrangement
which did not promote harmonious relations between
the burgesses and the Prior. At Estenhale, near
Sturbridge Green, the Canons owned both banks of
the river and claimed exclusive rights of fishing in
mid-channel, other folk having only the right to fish
so far as they could by wading up to the knees. Later,
between the Town and the Priory arose a dispute as
to the proprietorship of the ferry between Chesterton
and Sturbridge Fair. After the Dissolution Chesterton
manor passed into the hands of a townsman, Richard
Brakyn, formerly tenant of the Priory. How
this 'town' of Chesterton annoyed the University
authorities in the sixteenth century by the violent
assertion of its privileges of brawling, bear-baiting,
and play-acting, has to be told in a later chapter.

CHAPTER V.

Norman Cambridge

OF the character of Picot, the sheriff, there is a very sad account in the chronicle of Ely composed in the twelfth century by a certain monk named Thomas. ' A man by birth Norman, in mind Gaetulian '— terms synonymously abusive to English Thomas— ' a hungry lion, a ravening wolf, a filthy hog,' and so forth. His ultimate disappearance from Cambridge and assumed consignment to the nether world suggests a parallel with Dathan and Abiram. The front of his offending was that he had grabbed some land belonging to St Etheldreda's church. When remonstrance was attempted he profanely replied: ' Who is this Etheldreda whose lands, you say, I have snatched? I don't know anything about Etheldreda; and the lands I keep.'[1] Contrast the respectful language of the chronicler of Barnwell Priory, founded by the same Picot—' a man greatly enriched, as he well deserved, by the illustrious King William, with high honours and wealth in various parts of the realm ': of his migration to the realms of bliss he speaks with confidence.[2] So various are the estimates of Peter, the robbed, and Paul, the receiver of Peter's stolen goods.

But the endowment of the canons of St Giles, later established at Barnwell, was less the work of the ambiguous sheriff than of his devout wife, Hugolina. In the reign of William Rufus it happened that this lady was detained at Cambridge by illness so severe that the King's physicians, who had been summoned to attend her, pronounced her case desperate and abandoned her as at the point of death. Seeing that her only hope lay in divine assistance, she vowed that,

[1] *Liber Eliensis* ii. 131.　　　[2] *Liber Memorandorum* i. 38, 40.

if she were restored to health, she would build a church
in honour of her patron saint, Giles, and establish there
a religious household in his service. Her husband
consenting, she miraculously recovered. By the advice
of Archbishop Anselm and Bishop Remigius of Lincoln,
a church was built near the Castle at Cambridge, with
excellent dwellings for six canons of the regular or
Augustinian order.

Among the dotations of Picot to his canons was the
church of St Giles, ' where their house is founded.'
The words seem to imply that the church was already
in existence, and, so interpreted, they are justified
by the character of such remains of it as existed until
the old church was swept away in 1875, and of the
chancel arch which is retained in the new one. This
arch is of early Norman character, and dates from the
middle or latter part of the eleventh century. The
original church was very small, consisting of a nave,
without aisles, and a narrow chancel.

In process of time Robert, son of Picot, was charged
with conspiracy against Henry I, and anticipated
judgment by flight. The King confiscated the barony
conferred on Picot and bestowed it on a crusading
knight, one Pain Peverel. The ample endowment
provided for the canons by Picot seems to have failed ;
for when Pain Peverel visited his barony he found their
house desolate. The site moreover was confined and
contained no springs of water. Pain Peverel obtained
from King Henry a new site, described as very delight-
ful, in the Fields of Cambridge, on land between the
highway (Newmarket Road) and the river. He also
increased the number of the canons to thirty. The
Barnwell chronicler proceeds :

> Moreover in the middle of the place some springs, fresh and
> pure, welled forth, in English called Barnewelle, that is, the
> Children's Wells, at the time so called because once a year, on the
> Vigil of the Nativity of St John the Baptist, boys and youths used
> to meet there, and, as is the English habit, engaged in wrestling
> and other youthful games, and with songs and instruments of

music applauded each other.   So it happened that owing to the
multitude of boys and girls resorting thither for their sports it
became a custom for a crowd of merchants to meet there on the same
day to traffic and buy and sell.   Also in the same spot a man of
great sanctity, Godesone by name, had been wont to dwell, leading
a solitary life and possessing a tiny wooden oratory, dedicated
to the Apostle St Andrew.   He had lately died and left the place
without inhabitant and the oratory without a keeper.[1]

The translation of the canons to their new home took
place in 1112, twenty years after their establishment
under the Castle by Picot.   They proceeded to erect
'a church of great size and ponderous fabric.'   This
Norman church was removed and another 'more
beautiful' built in its place about the year 1200.[2]

Out of the casual gathering of merchants about the
Children's Wells grew up the Fair, still of some consequence, and held on June 22 and three following
days on the common land which, from the date at which
the Fair is held, is called Midsummer Common.   Of
the Cambridge fairs it is the first recorded and perhaps
the oldest.   Until the farm of the town was granted
to the burgesses by King John market tolls presumably
formed a part of the 'customs' of the Crown.   The
King parted with his rights in Midsummer Fair to the
Barnwell canons, and his grant was confirmed by
Henry III in 1229.   But the townspeople sued the
Prior and Canons, claiming that the tolls were included
in the farm granted to them by the King.   The
dispute was tried in an action at Huntingdon in 1232,
when it was decided that the Prior and Canons should
pay the townsmen a yearly quit-rent of half a mark

[1] The picturesque story of the games at the Children's Wells is discredited
by Professor Skeat as being based on a false etymology.   The oldest form of
the word, he says, is Bernewelle, or Beornwelle, which he derives from a
personal name beginning with *Beorn*—signifying 'a warrior.'   But the Barnwell
chronicler and the charter of Peverel, as quoted by him, spell it Barnewelle.
There is a Barnwell in Northamptonshire, and it would be odd if the wells in
both cases were associated with a personal name of a type not common.   The
connection of wells with popular sports is too well attested to be dismissed
as 'imaginary.'   At Clerkenwell, in London, as late as Stow's time, 'were
divers days spent in the pastime of wrestling,' as also at Skinner's Well.   In
the later middle ages interludes and Scriptural plays were annually performed
at several of the London wells.

[2] *Liber Memorandorum* i. 46, 66.

for any rights they might possess in the Fair. In 1506 the Corporation for a yearly rent of four marks acquired from the Priory the right of holding the Fair.

The Barnwell canons had been established in their new quarters some twenty years when two other religious houses were planted in the town. One of these was the Benedictine nunnery originally dedicated to St Mary, later to St Mary and St Radegund. The date of its foundation is uncertain; but as 'a little cell outside the town of Cambridge' it was already in existence when it was taken under the patronage of Nigellus, the second bishop of Ely (1133–1169). Among its earliest charters are those given by King Stephen and Constance, widow of Stephen's son, Eustace. One of the grants of Constance was immunity from hagable and landgable. As these were a part of the 'customs' of the town, and therefore a royal prerogative, it would seem that Cambridge was one of the towns usually assigned in dower to ladies of the royal family. Queen Catherine, wife of Charles II, was the last English queen who held the fee farm of Cambridge. The site on which the nunnery was built was called Grenecroft and, like that of Barnwell Priory, had been a part of the Common Field. Malcolm IV, King of Scotland, gave the nuns land whereon to build their church. He was Earl of Huntingdon, and perhaps in virtue of his office had acquired this bit of King's land. In comparison with their Barnwell neighbours, the St Radegund nuns were never opulent folk. But they built themselves a large church, which —though shorn of aisles, side-chapels and the best part of its nave—survives as the beautiful chapel of Jesus College. The transitional Norman work in the north transept belongs to King Malcolm's time, about 1160. The nuns had a small fair in their grounds on the vigil and feast of the Assumption (August 14, 15), for holding which they obtained a charter from King Stephen. In later days it was known as Garlic Fair, and it continued to be held in the grounds of Jesus College until the end of the eighteenth century.

The Hospital of St John in its birth and in its death was almost exactly coeval with the Nunnery of St Radegund, and, like it, was perpetuated in a College of the University. It was established by a burgess, named Henry Frost, for a community of regular or Augustinian canons, whose duty was to care for the poor and sick.[1] A few years earlier Rahere's Hospital —now St Bartholomew's—was founded in London, and was also served by Canons regular. The site assigned to the Cambridge Hospital was described in 1278 as a very poor and waste place belonging to the commonalty of the town. The statement is not historically accurate for, at the date of Frost's foundation, the waste of Cambridge borough was the property of the King. The situation was not attractive. Most of the ground between the old All Saints' church and the river was a swampy alluvium. The Chapel and Infirmary were built on artificially raised ground. This was the first foundation placed on the western side of the High Street, where now there is a continuous line of Colleges. The buildings of the Hospital suffered an unkinder fate than those of St Radegund. Such as were spared when they were converted to the uses of St John's College (1511) were ruthlessly destroyed in 1864 when the College cleared the site for its new chapel. The surviving witness of St John's Hospital is not the College which bears its name, but the oldest of Cambridge colleges, Peterhouse, which was a scion of the Hospital, planted in 1284 in another soil.

Another Hospital, that of St Mary Magdalene, or

---

[1] Such, at least, was the allegation of the burgesses, recorded in the Hundred Rolls, and they claimed the presentation to the Mastership of the Hospital. Hugh Northwold, Bishop of Ely (1220–54), gave a different account of the matter. According to him the Hospital was established by a certain Henry Eldcorn, of Cambridge, who built a very mean cottage to lodge the poor, and afterwards obtained from Bishop Eustace (1197–1215) license to establish there an oratory and burying ground, and from that time the patronage of the place belonged to the Bishops of Ely. The burgesses also complained that Bishop Northwold had alienated from them the appointment of the lepers' hospital at Sturbridge.

lepers, came into existence about the same time as that
of St John, and was also planted in the Common Field
of Cambridge. It stood, remote from houses, on the
extreme eastern verge of the borough. We do not
know when or by whom it was founded, nor to what
persons the care of the lepers was assigned, and it has
left no trace of domestic buildings. But there remains
by Barnwell station its remarkable little chapel, which
recently reverted to something like its original use
and served as the chapel of the Barnwell Military
Hospital. The appearance of the building points to
a date about 1125. Leprosy, never a common disease
in England, became rare after 1300, and leper houses
gradually disappeared or were converted to other uses.
In 1272 it was complained that the Warden of the
Cambridge house maintained no lepers, and that the
Bishop of Ely, within the last thirty years, had appropriated the presentation to the Hospital which
rightfully belonged to the burgesses. The chapel
may have been older than the Hospital, which is first
mentioned in 1199. King John, with all his faults,
was a notable patron of lepers. About the year 1211
he granted the Hospital a fair, to be held in its close
on the vigil and feast of the Holy Cross (September
13, 14). This was the celebrated Sturbridge Fair
described in letters patent of Queen Elizabeth (1589)
as 'by far the largest and most famous fair in all
England.' Out of the profits of this Fair the Corporation not only raised the greater part of the fee
farm due to the Crown, but also were able to repair
roads, streets and ditches. At an unknown date the
Corporation acquired or usurped the right of holding
the Fair, and in 1376 they passed an ordinance
forbidding any burgess to take the chapel to farm,
except to the use of the mayor and bailiffs, or to hold
market there, or make and let booths.

Yet another fair was recognised by a charter of King
John dated 1200. This granted to the burgesses,

for the amendment of their borough, to hold a fair in Rogation week with all the liberties which they had been accustomed to have. Evidently the Fair was already in existence at the time of the grant. There is an obscurity about the place of the Fair which I am unable to clear up. In the return which the town jurors made to King Edward I in 1278 it is distinctly stated that the fair was held ' in the town of Cambridge.' But at an inquisition held at Cambridge in 1388 the jurors affirmed that the Rogation Fair was then held at the hamlet of Reach in the township of Swaffham Prior, and that by the grant of the King's progenitors the Cambridge burgesses held two parts of it and the Prior of Ely one third part. Yet the jurors of the hundred of Stane, in which Reach is situated, alleged in 1278 that the two parts belonged not to the burgesses but to the King. Of a Rogation Fair at Cambridge there is no record after 1278, and there is nothing to show when the King parted with his shares to the burgesses. From time immemorial to the present day the Fair has always been held at Reach, and it is annually opened by the Mayor of Cambridge.

About fifty years after the Conqueror built his Castle the town once more changed its name, and thenceforth was called Cantebrig. How this change, which is not phonetic, came about it is hard to say. It may be observed that the Field of this northern town was called Cambridge Field to distinguish it from the Field south and east of the river which was generally known as Barnwell Field. Also that near the Castle Magdalene Street was once crossed by a watercourse called Cambrigge which was spanned by a bridge known as Cambrigge Brigg. We do not know what name or names the town, or the two parts of it, bore before 875. It is possible that the northern town was distinctively called Cantebrig, that the Castle being situated in that part was known as Cantebrig Castle, and that, after it was built, the name got transferred to the whole town.

THE NORTH-EAST VIEW OF CAMBRIDGE-CASTLE.

The Castle Hill and Gatehouse in 1730

CHAPTER VI.

The Freedom of the Borough

THE earliest of royal rescripts relating to Cambridge is an undated writ of Henry I ordaining that no ship shall discharge at any hithe in the shire except at Cambridge, and that toll shall be taken there, and there only. In making this enactment the King, no doubt, had a single eye to his own interest. The tolls were the King's tolls, and, for fiscal reasons, contraband trade at other ports was to be discouraged.[1] Nevertheless the carrying trade must have put money in the pockets of the townsmen. More important to them perhaps was another provision of the writ—'Whosoever doth forfeit in the borough let him there do right.' Where? Perhaps in the borough moot of the townsmen. If so it is a step towards autonomy. More probably it was in the sheriff's court, the profits of which made a part of the 'customs' of the town. But the townsmen were spared the expense and annoyance of having to resort to distant places for the settlement of their claims.[2]

'Customs' in Domesday Book very definitely means the customary dues of the Crown. But there is a 'custom' of which there is frequent mention in the writs and charters of monarchs who came after Henry I.

---

[1] In 1224 King Henry III ordered that corn ships trading to London should discharge their cargo only at the Queen's Hithe. As at Cambridge, the customs collected there originally formed part of the Queen's dowry.

[2] Nevertheless, it is on record that in 1324 at the fair court of Carnarvon, Henry Toft, of Cambridge, sued William Carbonel, a Cambridge bailiff, for a sum of money borrowed by the latter at Cambridge.

'Custom' is more ancient than the Conquest, more
potent than king's decrees. There is a 'free custom
of the borough,' mentioned in the earliest Cambridge
charter, which was 'ancient' in the days of King
John—some spark of independence kindled perhaps
before, perhaps after, the Conquest, which gener-
ations of sheriffs had not been able wholly to
extinguish.

Yet the two charters of King John (1201 and 1207)
are momentous in Cambridge history. They were
preceded by an undated writ of Henry II in which the
King delivered at farm to the burgesses his town of
Cambridge, to be held of him in chief by the same farm
as the sheriffs were wont to render to him. In 1185
the burgesses account to the Exchequer for 300 marks
of silver and one mark of gold that they may have the
town at farm, and that the sheriff shall not meddle
with it; again in 1220 they give 250 marks to have a
charter of liberties such as those contained in the charter
of Gloucester. Henry's writ is brief; there is nothing
in it to show that the grant was in perpetuity. King
John's second charter grants the town to the burgesses
'to hold for ever of us and our heirs to them and to
their heirs.' Though the Cambridge people deemed
it prudent to obtain confirmation of their immunities
from many of King John's successors, and though the
town is still the King's town, it is for ever free to
fashion itself after what pattern it wills.

Other important privileges are conveyed to the
burgesses in the King's first charter. They may have
a gild of merchants, all of whom are to be quit of tolls,
in fair and without, in all the King's lands on this side
of the sea and beyond it. All suits between burgesses
respecting money or lands are to be tried 'within the
borough according to the custom of the borough.'
They are granted their fair in Rogation week with its
liberties 'as they were accustomed to have it.' And,
vaguely, they are to enjoy 'all other liberties and

free customs which they had in the times of our predecessors.'

So far as concerns the Gild Merchant the charter might seem to have been a dead letter. The jurors in 1278 do indeed state that the burgesses have a Gild Merchant, but they are merely quoting King John's charter. Social and religious gilds were not a few at Cambridge: thirty-three are known to have existed at various times. The Thanes' Gild was older than the Conquest: a Gild of St Catherine met in the Priory Church at Barnwell and had a hall of its own; a Gild of the Holy Sepulchre built the Round Church; two other such Gilds—those of Corpus Christi and of St Mary in the Market Place—combined to endow the College of Corpus Christi in the fourteenth century; others were connected with various parish churches.[1] Craft gilds too there may have been: there was a Company of Cordwainers in the reign of Elizabeth, and the Tanners had a hall. But of a general Gild Merchant we hear nothing at all until the reign of Edward VI. Then (in 1547), when the town was interested in procuring a confirmation of its ancient charters, the assembled burgesses agree that ' all the free burgesses that now be, or hereafter shall be, shall be brethren of the Gild Merchant within this town.' It is scarcely to be questioned that this was their interpretation of King John's charter. Probably they were right: from the first the Gild Merchant was co-extensive with the whole burgess body. Every free-man, whether present or not, was required to contribute

---

[1] Miss Bateson (*Cambridge Guild Records*, Introduction xi.) says: 'Cambridge, whose contribution to the history of the "merchant" gild and of the "craft" gild is singularly poor, can provide examples of the "social-religious" gild in the eleventh, twelfth and thirteenth centuries; and this is unusual wealth. The story breaks off far oftener than the historian could wish, but in the continuity of its religious gild history Cambridge is likely to find no rival, unless it be Exeter.' Sometimes the Gild of St Mary was called the Gild of Merchants of the Blessed Virgin. Its earliest extant charters date from 1285; but, no doubt, it existed before then. May it, perhaps, be identified with the Gild Merchant of King John's charter? Probably not; for in 1547 it was asserted that all freemen were brethren of the Gild Merchant of the Town, and the Gild of St Mary had ceased to exist long before that year; moreover, it is unlikely that the Gild Merchant was of a religious pattern.

to the charge of the supper of the Gild Merchant, annually held on Bartholomew's night.[1] The place of meeting was indifferently called the Town Hall and the Gild Hall, and in 1555 it is stated that the Mayor was Alderman of the Gild Merchant.

In his second charter King John specifically includes in his concession 'meadows, pastures, mills, waters and pools.' This is perhaps not so much an addition to the former grant as an interpretation of it. All the soil within the borough limits—not merely the sites of houses and arable strips in the Field—passes into the tenure of the commonalty. With it passes the King's Mill. Its mere existence on the land of which Picot had robbed them was a grievance to the townsmen. Henceforth they will grind their corn at their own mill and pay no extortionate toll to the sheriff. It will always be the King's Mill—the Bishop of Ely had a mill next to it—for, though it is farmed by the townsmen, it is the King's in fee. The practical possession of the river is to be of more importance to the townspeople than the Mills. It includes fishing rights, which were valuable in times when meat was hard to come by. Down to the days of Charles II the Mayor and Aldermen, as an assertion of their right, used to 'go a-fishing according to custom' from Newnham 'pit' to the limit of the borough next Fen Ditton. In early times the fish of the fens and rivers were the staple commodity of the county. Rents were commonly paid in kind by delivery of a specified number of eels, and if the town would gratify a king,

---

[1] On Bartholomew's day (August 24) it was the custom for the new-elect Mayor to entertain the Council and freemen of the town at his house. Alderman Newton, in his Diary, describes the proceedings in 1668. A leading citizen of the town, Hervey fitz Eustace, who lived *circa* 1211, witnesses deeds as alternatively Mayor and Alderman, probably as combining the offices of Mayor of the Borough and Alderman of the Gild; there is no mention of aldermen of the borough before 1268. As was the case at London, there was probably a Gild Alderman before the town corporation had any existence. Aldermanbury, in London, and Alderman Hill, which was in Cambridge Field, witness to the antiquity of the title in either town. Though the court of the Gild Merchant had no organisation distinct from that of the Borough court, if we may trust royal letters of 1548, it sat at separate times, but only 'according to the exigence of the complaint.' (Bateson, *Charters of Cambridge Borough*, 85.)

a bishop or itinerating judge the obvious *douceur* was a present of fish.   Even more important than the fishing right was the river trade.   Throughout its length within the borough the river on either bank was fringed by the common land which under their charter the townspeople freely enjoyed.   On the town-ward side numerous hithes arose, the soil of which was rented from the town, though they came to be known by the names of the merchants who used them— Dame Nicol, Cholles, &c.—or by the commodities wared there, as Cornhithe, Salthithe.   To serve these hithes and the Mills a new street, called Milne Street, was made on artificially raised ground between the Mills and what is now the Great Court of Trinity; and many lanes crept down from it to the river.

Two things within the natural bounds of the borough the townsmen did not acquire, and would much rather not acquire—the Castle and the Bridge.   These are matters pertaining to the national defence, and have always been, and will be, the concern of kings.   Indeed the Castle is not in Cambridge borough, but in the county and in Chesterton parish.   King John in his charters makes no mention of either, for the well-under-stood reason that the maintenance of both is a charge on the county, or on particular estates in it, and not on the borough.   At the Castle the sheriff remains— now so far as the burgesses are concerned, a Giant Pope, biting his nails because he cannot come at them. There he has his gaol for rural misdoers, and to it for centuries to come intractable scholars may be com-mitted by the University authorities.   The townsmen have their separate gaol, next the Tolbooth, in the house which once belonged to Benjamin the Jew, and was granted to them for that use by Henry III in 1224.

With the custody of the Castle went that of the Great Bridge.   I do not think that the Great Bridge is in any parish of Cambridge.   As the sheriff continued to receive pontage rents from county landowners

D

it was his duty to see to the repair of the Bridge—
a duty which at all times was scandalously neglected.
It was the constant complaint of the townsmen that the
Bridge was *debilis fractus et dissolutus.* In 1273 a
great flood happened, and the water is said to have
risen five feet above the Bridge, which no doubt suffered
total or partial dissolution.[1] Here was the sheriff's
opportunity. The pontage tax was legally sixpence
for each hide (120 acres) of the lands subject to the
levy: he raised it to two shillings, promising that he
would build a new bridge of stone. But all that he
did was to tinker at the old affair with timber and
hurdles, and during the repairs he made a clean profit
by starting a ferry for which he exacted toll. The
keeper of the sheriff's prison—doubtless at his master's
suggestion—actually took away by night planks provided for repairs, in order to delay the work and increase
the sheriff's profits. The vehicles of ‘ magnates ’ and
others constantly fell into the river and were got out
with difficulty. As time went on trouble arose with
the county taxpayers. When the military use of
the bridge became of secondary importance they
raised constant objections to an impost which contributed principally to the benefit of the town, and down
to the middle of the eighteenth century there was
recurrent difficulty in getting in the pontage money.
The new bridge of stone which was constructed in
1754 was built by public subscription. The present
iron bridge dates from 1823. The county magistrates
superintended its erection, but the cost was almost
entirely defrayed by private contributions with but
small assistance from the Town Corporation.

The ‘ customs ’ of the town—whatever was included
in them—amounted in 1086 to seven pounds, and the
landgable, or rents for holdings in the Fields, to a
rather larger sum: there was besides a considerable
amount of untaxed waste. The charter of 1207 states

[1] Chronicle of John de Oxenedes, 221 (Rolls Series).

that the 'ancient farm,' hitherto collected by the sheriff, was £40, to which the king added £20 of increase. Later—it does not appear exactly when—the sum was raised to 101 marks, and after the Peasants' Rising in 1381 it was again increased to 105 marks, or £70, which from that time remained the constant rate.[1] In 1671 the reversion of this rent, which was at the time enjoyed by the Queen of Charles II, was purchased by Sir George Downing, and by the will of his grandson, another Sir George, it passed into the revenues of Downing College.

To one question we must find an answer before we dismiss King John's charters. Who are the burgesses to whom the town and its appurtenances are granted? The answer, I think, is—every man who by his tenure of house or land within the borough had formerly paid hagable or landgable to the sheriff and henceforth pays it to the commonalty. In process of time several houses might be built on a plot where one had stood in the time of Domesday, and in such cases the original tenement seems to have been charged with hagable for the whole site; in return the owner had special privilege in using the common pasture. On the other hand several adjoining strips in the arable Field were often merged in one, and so individuals, and more often religious corporations, came to be relatively large owners in the Field.

A clause in the earlier charter directs that if any in all the King's lands shall take toll or customs of men of the Gild Merchant of Cambridge, then either the sheriff or the reeve (*prepositus*) of Cambridge shall take distress thereof at Cambridge. The reeve is evidently no newly constituted official but an already existing representative of the burgesses, the *port-gerefa* of days before the Conquest. In days to come he will get the title of *major ballivus*, or mayor, chief

---

[1] In the accounts of the unreformed Corporation in 1832 the sum charged as fee farm rent is £61 5s. 0d.; apparently the mark was reckoned at 11s. 8d., instead of 13s. 4d.

of the bailiffs of the town. The evolution of a Corporation at Cambridge has no witness in the earlier royal charters: to the last days of the Plantagenets it is vaguely and indifferently styled 'the men' or 'the burgesses,' or the 'mayor and bailiffs' of Cambridge. In 1530 Cambridge asserted its claim to be a borough by prescription. Not until 1605 did it obtain royal letters patent creating it 'a body corporate by the name of the mayor, bailiffs and burgesses of the borough of Cambridge.' Even then King James left matters as he found them and set up no constitution for the borough, nor any council to rule it.

Of the gradual evolution of the burghal constitution, unnoticed by princes, there are but faint traces in the municipal records. In his charter of 1201 King John mentions 'the reeve of Cambridge' as its presiding officer. The first mention of a mayor and bailiffs is in a writ of Henry III, dated 1231, and in the same writ we discover that another corporation has arisen in the town calling itself the Chancellor and Masters of the University of Cambridge. This is a matter to disquiet the municipal heart for long centuries. In their midst has arisen a powerful Gild which is altogether outside the control of the civic authorities and unremittingly hostile to them. The occasion of the writ was the presence in the town of disorderly persons, claiming to be scholars, who disturbed the King's peace. Affrays between 'clerks' and laymen were constantly recurrent and the townsmen were powerless to punish the former. Authority to imprison or release offending scholars was taken out of their hands and given to the Chancellor, and at his request the detested sheriff was required to confine them, not in the town-gaol, but at the Castle. In 1268 the King was at Cambridge, and to compose the differences between the two bodies he issued a writ to the town defining, within certain limits, its relations with the University. To assist the mayor and bailiffs in keeping the peace there are to be associated with them two aldermen and four of the more discreet burgesses. These officials are only peace officers.

The bailiffs are four in number. At Norwich there were also four, each of them chosen by one of the four districts which composed the city. Whether the Cambridge four were originally so apportioned is not clear. In later times they were called bailiffs of the Tolbooth, the Mills, the Bridge, and the High Ward respectively. With the mayor they constitute the borough court where wills bequeathing lands within the liberties are proved, and demises and leases are witnessed. In the borough court they determine in contracts between burgesses. They collect fines, rents, tolls, paving money, &c., and generally take the place of the sheriff in intra-mural matters.

In process of time the distinction between bailiffs and aldermen ceased to be regarded, though the original four were sometimes known as ' the ancient aldermen.' The number of aldermen was gradually increased and was finally fixed at twelve.

The mode of electing the mayor, the four bailiffs, the two aldermen, the four burgesses (called councillors), and the two taxors, was far removed from modern ideas of democratic control, though it corresponded with the practice of most ancient boroughs. One man was nominated by the mayor, a second by the commonalty. These two elected twelve men of the commonalty, who in turn elected six others, and the eighteen—the two originally selected being excluded from a voice—chose the officers of the coming year. Afterwards the number of electors was increased to twenty-four, who as ' the Twenty-four ' constituted the Common Council of the town. This curious method, with occasional intermissions and variations in detail, lasted until the passing of the Municipal Reform Act of 1835.[1]

[1] For the significance of the early charters the important Introduction of Professor Maitland to Bateson's *Charters of Cambridge Borough*, xv.–xix., should be consulted.

A similar plan was adopted in the choice of burgesses to represent the Town in Parliament. Cambridge has returned its representatives continuously since the first genuine Parliament, that of 1295. The electors were a selected body of burgesses, usually eight in number. In 1503 the method was that the mayor and commonalty each chose one man, which two chose eight others, and the eight elected the two burgesses in Parliament. This plan continued until 1625, when, apparently for the first time, the election was 'by the greatest number of the burgesses.' The two representatives were paid by the Town at the rate of one shilling a day for the time when their duties called them away from Cambridge.

Before the date of King John's first charter individual burghers are innominate and indistinguishable, or, at most, 'antecessors,' or progenitors of men who left something besides their names to remember. After 1200 names can be clothed in something like flesh and blood. Quite the most considerable citizen in the days of John and Henry III was a certain Hervey, son of Eustace, otherwise Hervey the Alderman. His seal indicates that he was of knightly rank, and he proved his military prowess in 1200 by challenging a member of the Picot family to wager of battle in respect of some land at Gamlingay ; which offer his antagonist declined on the ground of bodily infirmity.[1] He was of the family of Dunning, which in the thirteenth century was one of the richest in the town. They occupied the house which in times comparatively recent has got the name, School of Pythagoras, though it never had any connection with Cambridge University. As a 'stone house' among mud-built neighbours it proclaimed the exceptional wealth of its owners : for in those days only Jews and dignitaries of the Church were rich enough to build houses of stone. Not all the mayors

---

[1] 'Duel,' or wager of battle, between burgesses was forbidden in the charter of 1227.

SCHOOL OF PYTHAGORAS IN 1842

and bailiffs were men of repute. One of them, Roger of Withersfield, was so unfortunate as to be hanged for murder in 1290, and two others, convicted for the same crime, only escaped the same fate by claiming benefit of clergy. It is to be remarked that of the mayors of the thirteenth and fourteenth centuries, besides these two, six at least were ' clerks,' *i.e.* apparently members of the University—evidence that there was no impassable gulf between Town and Gown.

CHAPTER VII.

The Islanders and the Friars

THE historian of Cambridge is well equipped with documentary materials for illustrating its internal and domestic history. But of events that happened at Cambridge, there are very few that touch the fringe of national history, and of those few hardly any have much bearing on the fortunes of the town. Its deserted castle and broken bridge exemplify the small importance attached to it by later Plantagenet kings as a military stronghold, and its river, leading to nothing but Cambridge, marks it as situated on a backwater, remote from the wider current of national affairs.

Yet one conspicuous event in the reign of Henry III served to flush the normally quiet stream of Cambridge life, and when the flood receded it left some lasting marks of its passage. The first Castle was built by the Conqueror after his reduction of the Isle of Ely: to provide defence against trouble from the same quarter Edward I began a new Castle about the year 1283. The Barons, defeated at Evesham in 1265, made their last stronghold in the Isle, and in the following year marauding bands issued thence and ravaged the surrounding country. The Barnwell annalist paints some vivid pictures of that troublous year—not without some malicious enjoyment of the ridiculous straits to which his religious superiors were reduced.

First the raiders attacked a manor belonging to the Barnwell Canons at Wiggenhall in Norfolk. The Prior, Jolanus of Thorney, was at the time on a visit there, attended by a large troop with horses and harness. Assaulted by the brigands the Prior and his men escaped in great fright, ' some through windows, some over walls,' and, unaccompanied, the Prior took refuge in Dereham Abbey. ' And the aforesaid robbers took away all the Prior's horses and harness, leaving only one veteran horse,' of which a tragi-comical history is told later, ' and putting on the Canon's rain-copes, in derision of them and their order, made loud laughter and mockery.' Worse followed. The Barons carried off rich men, especially Jews, to the Isle and held them to ransom.[1] They made prey of sheep and oxen, corn and malt—everything they could lay hands on. Some of the country-folk arrested a certain ' ribald ' Islander and cut off his head. The Islanders retaliated by burning, among other places, a manor of the Priory at Bourn in Cambridgeshire, and certain ' ministers of iniquity ' quartered themselves in the Priory itself, eating, drinking and destroying. The poor Canons made what show of hospitality they could, eating and drinking with them and always in doubt that worse was to come. A certain man ' of great stature,' called Philip the Champion—' bruiser,' as we should call him—roused the Prior from his bed at daybreak. ' I am going to have all your corn, all your malt, all your larder. Hand over the keys.' ' If that's so,' said the Prior, ' there's no stopping here for us.' Two friends of the Prior came to his relief and remonstrated. To whom Philip replied, ' I am going to take the lot, in the teeth of you.' To which they made answer, ' By God's wounds, you shall not,' and swords were drawn on both sides; but bystanders interfered, and in a rage the spoilers withdrew without effecting their purpose.

[1] In the *Vetus Liber* of the Archdeacons of Ely there is a Calendar in which there is a note of a massacre (*interfectio*) of Jews at Cambridge on August 12, 1266. In 1817 workmen digging in the cellar of the Dolphin inn discovered an old leathern bag containing rings, jewels and silver pennies, several of them struck in the fifty-first year of Henry III (1266). As the Dolphin was situated in what had been the Old Jewry, it would appear that the treasure had been hidden by a Jew.

When the King heard of the proceedings of the Islanders he came to Cambridge with a great army and there lodged. His brother, Richard, 'King of Almain,' was entertained in the Priory. The King caused gates to be made and ditches encompassing the town, in such haste that the work-people were not allowed to rest even on saints' days. Unfortunately the King, hearing that the Earl of Gloucester had seized London, hastily withdrew with his army, leaving Cambridge defenceless. Thereupon the Islanders came with a great host and burnt the gates and the houses in which the King had lodged. The townsmen fled, leaving not a soul to resist them. At Barnwell the raiders were only prevented from burning the Hall, where the King of Almain had been entertained, by the interposition of two Peche brothers, who swore that they would rather die than allow the tombs of their ancestors, benefactors of the Priory, to be burnt.

Then a troublesome lord, one John de Burgh of Harston, sent an imperative request to Prior Jolanus for the loan of a war-horse. Of all his stable the only horse remaining to the Prior was the 'veteran' steed, 'tall and bony,' which the outlaws had spared at Wiggenhall; and this he sent. 'On seeing it John and his company cried, "Where did you get this crazy old devil?" And with loud laughter they came about the aforesaid horse, some showing its teeth, some feeling its head and back, some dragging the poor creature by the tail, some pricking it and making it kick. Some said " Skin it," others " Burn it," and John sent it back with a message. "I don't greet you, and I don't thank you for the loan of your old horse. Now send me a good trotting palfrey, not as a loan but as a gift; and send a reply by the bearer at once." The Prior, considering the times and the person, was careful to send a humble answer. "I wish I could send you a serviceable palfrey. Once I had palfreys; now I will send such as I can." So he bought a new palfrey, rather small, but a good goer, and sent it, and John never sent it back.' Little wonder that after such humiliations the Prior fell ill, and the Bishop of Ely and William Peche, ' patron ' of the Priory, appeared together at Barnwell and insisted on his resignation.

The gates which the King made were the two called Barnwell Gates and Trumpington Gates—the former between the Post Office and Christ's College, the latter at the crossing of Trumpington Street and Pembroke Street. The gates burnt by the Islanders were later constructed anew, and are often referred to in leases of properties of the thirteenth and fourteenth centuries. Dr Caius mentions that one post remained in his day (about 1560) to mark where the Barnwell Gates stood; in the reign of Henry VII there were two, known as St Andrew's stulpes.[1]

The King's Ditch, which as a vaulted, underground channel, exists in a large part of its course at the present day, began at the pool below the Mills. It was carried along the northern side of Mill Lane and Pembroke Street to St Andrew's Hill; diverged from the street and passed through open ground to Barnwell Gates; then along Hobson Street and through the grounds of Sidney College; crossed Jesus Lane under a vault, and, continuing to the end of Park Street, rejoined the river near the Electric Works. It did not take its name from King Henry III, for in a deed of 1250 there is mention of a King's Ditch which served as the boundary of the close of the nuns of St Radegund. All that Henry III did in 1268 was to repair and deepen an existing channel, probably made by King John in 1200, when he reimbursed the bailiffs for their costs in ' enclosing ' the town. Pembroke Street in early times was called Langrithe Lane, *i.e.* the lane of the long channel. When the Ditch was no longer needed as a defence it fell into neglect, and already

[1] ' Bridge Ward Within, so called of London Bridge, beginneth at the stulpes on the south end by Southwark' (Stow's *London*).

in 1278 the townsmen complained of it as a nuisance. Encroachments on its banks were common : one man plants trees there, another spans it with a drawbridge. As it became a receptacle for all manner of filth it soon became a danger to the public health. In 1331 the University petitioned Parliament to compel the mayor and bailiffs to scour it : in 1348 a commission was issued to enquire what ought to be its breadth and who was bound to cleanse it. In 1574 the Vice-Chancellor, Dr Perne, in consequence of the danger of plague, mooted a plan for cleansing it by bringing into it water from Trumpington Ford, near the Botanic Garden. In 1610 the Town and University jointly carried out this plan by making a ' new river ' from the Nine Wells in Great Shelford parish to Trumpington Ford, and so along the street to the King's Ditch at the corner of Pembroke College. Until the early part of last century the open stream, which is a pleasant feature of Trumpington Street, did not skirt, as it now does, the eastern kerb, but was carried along the middle of the street, to the peril of careless drivers.

In 1209, two years after the date of King John's second charter, we hear for the first time of the existence at Cambridge of a large body of scholars. Probably their arrival may be assigned to a somewhat earlier time. It so nearly synchronises with the coming of the Friars that it seems possible that the one event had some connection with the other. The older monastic orders took little or no part in the establishment of the University. There is no evidence that the Austin canons at Barnwell interested themselves at all in the doings of the early scholars ; they embezzled a sum of money left to the University by a Bishop of Ely in 1257, of which they were trustees. The Hospital brethren quarrelled with the scholars. The great houses of the Benedictines at Ely, Crowland, Thorney, and Ramsey, never realised the advantage of their proximity to the University until a much later age. But the Friars, both at their first coming and in after times, showed their friendliness to the scholars and eagerness to profit by their learning.

The first to arrive were the Franciscans, or Grey Friars, in 1224. They settled in a place called the Old Synagogue, where the burgesses granted them a site next their prison.[1] This prison was in Butter Row, adjoining the present Guildhall. It had been the house of a Jew, Benjamin, and was granted by the King to the burgesses to serve as a gaol in the very year of the arrival of the Franciscans. The prison and the Friars' house had a common entrance—an arrangement so intolerable that the brethren secured another site from the King and there built a chapel so humble that a single carpenter finished it in one day. Some fifty years later they moved to a new site consisting of six acres, now contained in the grounds of Sidney College, and there built a church. They also built themselves a very large hall, described by Ascham in 1540 as an ornament to the University, which, having then no suitable building of its own, there held its congregations and meetings for business.

The Franciscans were followed in 1249 by the Carmelite or White Friars. Originally they settled at Chesterton in a place called the Carme. Afterwards they removed to Newnham and built a church, cloister, dormitory, and cells, and there remained for forty years. Then, about the year 1290, finding that they suffered great inconvenience from winter floods, which prevented the scholars from attending lectures in their house and the brethren from going into the town, they removed to the parish of St John in Milne Street, to a site now occupied partly by the grounds of

---

[1] When the foundations of the Guildhall were dug in 1782 several gravestones were discovered, one of which bore an imperfect Hebrew inscription: 'The gravestone of Israel . . . who died . . .' It is not recorded that there was a synagogue in the Jewry, which was near the old All Saints Church. Jews sometimes had permission to live outside the Jewry. In 1277 the sheriff is directed to permit Joceus, the Jew, to dwell in Chesterton, so that he might have access to Cambridge to ply his merchandise there and to repair the houses that he had in the town (Close Rolls).

Queens' College, partly by the Lodge of the Provost of King's College.

Next came some minor orders: the Bethlehemite Friars, the only house of this order in England, who made their home in Trumpington Street in 1257; the Friars of Penitence, or the Sack, first established in the parish of St Mary at the Market, but afterwards removed to the site of Peterhouse; and the Friars of St Mary, who settled in a street called Catton Rewe, in the parish of All Saints next the Castle. These three orders were suppressed in or soon after 1307. It is on record that the Friars of the Sack were very numerous and had among them many good scholars.

The next comers (about 1275) were the Black, Dominican, or Preaching Friars, who bequeathed their name to Preachers Street, as St Andrew's Street was called until Emmanuel College was built on the site of their house. Next in time (1290) were the Austin Friars, who occupied a wide area now comprised in the site of the University Laboratories, between Peas Hill, Free School Lane, Pembroke Street, and Corn Exchange Street. The gates of their convent, where Messrs. Barclays' Bank now stands, were in existence in the early years of the eighteenth century. In the same year (1290) came the White Canons of the order of St Gilbert of Sempringham. They settled next a chapel dedicated to St Edmund on the east side of Trumpington Street, nearly opposite Peterhouse. This household was established at Cambridge with the express object of enabling brethren of the order to study theology. Among its members in the thirteenth century were Alexander, brother of King Robert Bruce, and Robert Mannyng, well known for his metrical *Storie of Inglande.*

Chapter VIII.

The Coming of the Clerks

In the year 1376 the number of persons in Cambridge above fourteen years of age who were charged to Poll tax was 1722; the total population of the town was probably something more than 3000. In 1587 the number of inhabitants, apart from University residents, was stated to be 4990. A house to house return of the several parishes in 1749 showed the population at that time to be 6131. A similar return in 1794 stated the number as 9063.

Judged by the number of its inhabitants Cambridge, before the nineteenth century, was not a place of much consequence. But population is not the only index of the importance of a town, and Sturbridge Fair gave to Cambridge an eminence, as a centre of commerce, which may be compared with that of Nijni Novgorod in present times. But incomparably greater than Sturbridge Fair at the zenith of its glory, more enriching to the burgesses and ennobling to their town was the great Market of Learning whose traffic drew merchandizers from all England and parts beyond it. This is the History of Cambridge Town; but as the story of Sturbridge Fair and the bickerings which it entailed between the townsfolk, the tollers and the traders cannot be put outside the history, so, and more closely inwoven in it, is the narrative of the relations of the Town with the University and the age-long struggle of either corporation to assert its independence of the other.

Into this small town, as yet unemancipated from the sheriff, about the beginning of the thirteenth century there tumbled a mob of ' clerks.' Exactly when and wherefore they found their way to Cambridge we cannot say; but they came suddenly and they brought no good character. When some hundreds of them alighted there from Oxford, in 1209, there was an ugly tale of homicide as the cause of their flight from that University town. With not remote recollections of Constitutions of Clarendon and the immunity claimed for criminous clerks the townspeople looked with justifiable apprehension on this invasion. Benefit of clergy could be claimed by any man who could read: at his best the scholar was a wanderer, kinless and generally moneyless; and at the heels of the genuine student came a host of 'ribalds,' whose pretence of learning was a cloak for mendicancy and lawlessness. Moreover in every country of Europe the bearing of the medieval scholar towards the 'rustics' of the town in which he followed his studies was in the last degree provocative. Chaucer's two tales of the clerks of Cambridge and Oxford present the traditional attitude of the University man towards his town neighbours. The Miller of Trumpington defrauds the scholars, and they turn the tables on him by an invasion of his domestic peace; the scholar of Oxenford plays a trick on the carpenter with whom he lodges, makes love to his wife, and puts to rout his rival, the parish clerk. The scholars went about with daggers and bows and arrows. Riots, with attendant house-breakings and bloodshed, were kindled from any spark; and when the clerks had done with the townsmen they fought among themselves. The Chancellor and Masters of the University were wholly without authority to deal with offenders against academic discipline. And on their part they had much to allege against the townsmen. The sudden influx of the scholars, no doubt, had legitimately enhanced the prices of victual and lodging. The scholars lived in the houses of burghers or in hostels hired from them, and the University complained that extortionate rents were demanded.

Almost the only knowledge we have of the University
in the reign of Henry III relates to the constant
collisions of the townsmen with the clerks and consequent appeals to the King to compose their differences and execute justice on offenders. In 1231 the
King directed the sheriff to punish contumacious
scholars by imprisonment in the county gaol or banish-
ment from the town; but only at the discretion of the
Chancellor and Masters of the University. In the
eyes of the burghers this must have seemed a restoration
of the sheriff's interference in their affairs and an invasion of the liberties which they had purchased with
hard cash only a few years before; and their pockets
were touched by another order directing that the rents
of all hostels in which scholars lived should be assessed
by two Masters and two men of the town, appointed for
the purpose and called taxors.

The University taxors continued to exist until 1856.
They tested weights and measures. They took toll
of victuallers of the town and in Chesterton and pulled
down the signs of unlicensed alehouses. Along with
the town searchers they assayed wares offered at Sturbridge Fair and shared with the Town the fines resulting
therefrom. They measured coal and grain delivered
at the Quayside and gauged tuns. The University
bushel and instrument for testing casks are still to be
seen at the Registry.

But the grievance which beyond all others rankled
in the burgess heart was the right of ' conusance,' *i.e.*
the privilege given to the Chancellor and Masters of
trying all cases, civil or criminal, in which a clerk
was either plaintiff or defendant. This was quite a
different matter from the disciplinary powers in respect
of its students which were given to the University in
1231. When the Chancellor's Court was first constituted and what authority could be cited for its
powers is matter of doubt: they seem to have been regarded as inherent in the constitution of any University

E

and capable of enforcement in any place outside the University. The theory, stated in the *Historical Register*, that the University derived its powers from a charter dated 1305, is hardly correct. In 1288 certain Cambridge scholars being imprisoned in the Tower of London the Chancellor asserted and was allowed the claim that they should be delivered to him in accordance with the privilege of a University. In 1668 the University decreed that should any person enjoying its privilege be sued in the King's Courts at Westminster he should be defended at the charges of the University, and that any persons who should violate the privileges of the University by suing elsewhere than in the Chancellor's Court should be treated as the most noxious enemies of the University. As recently as 1848 the University 'discommuned' a Cambridge tradesman for suing in the ordinary Courts a Bachelor of Arts who was then resident in Yorkshire. Such proceedings seemed to the townsmen a virtual denial of legal remedy. Five centuries of Mr Cooper's *Annals of Cambridge* are filled with their groans and petitions to King or Parliament against the inequitable holding of the scales against them in the Chancellor's Court. Their prayers fell on deaf ears; the higher powers were always on the side of the scholars, and as the ages proceeded their chains were rivetted ever more tightly. The University men gloried in their tyranny: they called their Court 'the Townsmen's Scourge.' On a certain occasion 'the Mayor going about to repress misdemeanours offered by divers young men of the University was assaulted and evil intreated by three or four scholars, and his gown rent and spoiled, and some used lewd speeches to him, and he put in danger of his life. And the scholars being complained upon, answer was made by some University officers that they could not amend it, for so it hath been and so it will be still.'

It greatly added to the bitterness of the townsfolk

that the jurisdiction of the University was extended so
as to include a large number of residents in the town
who were not scholars.   It was long a matter for contention who should be accounted as 'privileged' to
claim asylum in the Chancellor's Court.   In 1503 it
was agreed between the Town and the University that
in the number of such persons should be included
(1) all menials receiving wages from scholars, (2) all
apothecaries, stationers, limners, scriveners, parchment-
makers, bookbinders, physicians, surgeons, and barbers
in the University, (3) all persons dwelling in the households of scholars or of scholars' servants.   The total
of individuals was about seventy.   In a charter to the
Town, dated 1589, it was limited that no Head of a
House should have more than two privileged retainers
dwelling in the town, and no University official more
than one, and that no such retained servant should
have goods exceeding £3 in value in the ward in which
he dwelt.   But husbands of College laundresses, and
College receivers and bailiffs were allowed to be privileged.   It was further complained by the townsmen
that many of the scholars, abandoning their studies
and taking on them the lay habit, set up in business
in the town as drapers, mercers, grocers, innholders,
&c., and, although they got great riches, refused to
undertake any of the duties falling on burgesses or to
contribute to the general charges of the town.

Each corporate body was constantly on the alert to
check the other from encroaching on its prerogatives,
and rigidly boycotted any of its members who sued in
the hostile Court.   In 1648 a burgess was fined by
the Corporation for suing before the Vice-Chancellor
contrary to the order of the Town; and in 1583 a
Fellow of King's was expelled the University for having
prosecuted a Master of Arts 'before foreign judges.'
Matters were worsened by the existence of two rival
Courts in Sturbridge Fair for determining pleas and
controversies concerning the sale of victuals; and

strangers to the town, if they so preferred, might bring their action before the University Commissary.

In the year 1261 there was an outbreak of more than usual violence between the townsmen and the scholars. Houses were plundered and the records of the University were burnt. The King thereupon issued a commission for the trial of the offenders. In the result sixteen townsmen were executed, others received lighter punishment or fled to sanctuary; twenty-eight of the scholars were found guilty, but received the King's pardon.[1] As has been already stated, in 1268 the King for the peace and advantage of the University issued a charter providing that there should be two aldermen in Cambridge and four discreet and lawful burgesses who should take oath to assist the Mayor and bailiffs in preserving the King's peace. It was further ordained that two men should be chosen from each parish to enquire for suspected persons in the parish: also that any layman who assaulted a clerk should be arrested and imprisoned until satisfaction should be made, but that if the assailant was a clerk the Chancellor might demand his release. In 1270, on the initiative of Prince Edward, a further agreement was arrived at. A body of ten scholars and ten burgesses was constituted who bound themselves by oath to cause the peace of the University to be kept: they were annually to be chosen within fifteen days of the Feast of St Michael, when the clerks resumed their lectures. The two bodies thus constituted seem from the first to have been united in one, which was known as the Great Congregation or Black Assembly; and with them were associated the Mayor, the four

[1] The riot originated in a dispute between the northern and southern scholars. Robert de Driffield, a northerner, and his fellows complain to the King that certain malefactors, clerks as well as lay, broke their inns, beat and plundered them. There was complaint, apparently among the townsfolk, of the injustice of the sentence of the visiting judges. The King, learning that 'the hands of affliction had been extended to one party more than was deserved, and no enquiry made of the other party, which was, perhaps, author of the trespass,' directs other judges to investigate, 'but not to the hanging or mutilation of clerks, but that they be chastised in some other way by the counsel of the University' (Patent Rolls).

bailiffs and the two Town taxors. It was a special indignity, deeply resented by the civic authorities, that at the October meeting in the Guildhall the University authorities, while they declined for themselves the oath to keep the peace, devised such a form of oath ' as made most for their appetite and pleasures,' and compelled the Town representatives to take it. Thereby they were bound ' to observe and keep the liberties and customs of the University '—a phrase which was capable of elastic interpretation. Many times the Mayor and Town officers refused the oath or declined to attend the meeting; but always the University was able to enforce their submission.

It would be tedious and profitless to rehearse the long struggle of the Town to emancipate itself from the shackles of University control laid upon it in the thirteenth century. The privilege which kings had created and legislators denied to remove was submerged by the process of time and the rising tide of municipal independence. The Black Assembly sank into desuetude before the close of the eighteenth century; a last and ineffectual attempt to resuscitate it was made by Dr Wood, Vice-Chancellor in 1817. The right of assaying victuals, which had been taken from the Town, and given to the University in 1381, and reserved to the latter by Act of Parliament so recently as 1836, was in practice dropped. The Municipal Corporations Act of 1835, which abolished the old oligarchic government of the borough and substituted for it a representative Council with extensive powers, did much to hasten the day of complete autonomy for the Town, though it professed to retain the privilege of the University. By the Cambridge Award Act of 1856 the University was deprived of its powers of granting alehouse licenses, of supervising weights and measures, of controlling markets and fairs, and—most important of all—its right of conusance. Its powers of arrest and imprisonment in the case of

' common women, procuresses, vagabonds, and other persons suspected of evil, coming or resorting to the town,' were surrendered by amicable negotiation between the Borough Council and the University in 1894, and at the same time the Vice-Chancellor's right of refusing consent to theatrical or other entertainments in the town was abandoned.

In the eighteenth century Lord Mansfield pronounced that the chartered jurisdiction of the University Court was essential to the happiness of the University. In the nineteenth century Lord Chief Justice Coleridge considered that its privileged existence was appropriate only to a state of things which was past. With that state of things much else has disappeared which belonged to the happiness of neither Town nor University. No longer does the Vice-Chancellor demand and the Mayor refuse the corporal oath which was the badge of municipal servitude. University ' clerks ' are proud to accept, as the Townsmen are glad to confer on them, the mayoral dignity, and as aldermen or councillors they share the responsibilities of governing the town of which they are burgesses; and in the Borough Court magistrates drawn from either body dispense justice without respect of persons.

CHAPTER IX.

The Black Death and the Peasants' Rising

IN spite of constant affrays of the scholars there can be little doubt that the town of Cambridge grew and greatly prospered in the century and a half following 1200. Its new liberties, the presence in it of some hundreds of scholars, the growth of its monastic houses and the great attraction of its fairs, undoubtedly gave it a consequence beyond that of most provincial towns. Though the originally rural character of the town was still witnessed at the close of the thirteenth century by the existence in its midst of many open spaces, shops and booths produced far more real wealth than granges. Beyond the town gates and the King's Ditch the house-covered area extended along the main thoroughfares for a distance which was not exceeded until the end of the eighteenth century. Intensively the growth was still more considerable. A row of hithes grew up between the Bridge and the Mills, and a new quarter of the town came into existence between the High Street and the river.

An indication of rising trade importance was the settlement of a Jewish community in the neighbourhood of the church of All Saints, which for that reason, and to distinguish it from the similarly dedicated church near the Castle, was commonly called All Saints in the Jewry. Jews must have settled in Cambridge not long after the Conquest, for about the middle of the twelfth century we find Nigellus, second Bishop of Ely, pawning a silver cross to the Cambridge Jews.[1] They were wealthy and lived in houses whose rental

[1] Wharton, *Anglia Sacra* i. 625. In a document of 1241 (Close Rolls) there is a list of Cambridge Jews; one of them was a son of *Magister* Levi, probably a University graduate.

shows that they were greatly superior to those of the ordinary townsmen. Besides their dwellings they had considerable property within the borough. In the treasury of Peterhouse there was, till recently, a bond, dated 1265, and written in Hebrew characters, of one Abraham, son of Samuel, quit-claiming certain land outside Trumpington Gates. Their wealth, and a suspicion of sharp practice attending it, made them highly unpopular. For the offence of coin-clipping, commonly laid at the door of the Jews, the house of one of them was confiscated to the King. In grants of property within the borough it was a common stipulation that it should not be transferred to the Jews. In the disturbances of 1266 they were special sufferers; numbers of them were carried into captivity and compelled to ransom themselves at excessive rates, and the King was obliged to issue letters patent calling on the Mayor and bailiffs to maintain and protect them. Norman and Angevin kings found in the fines imposed on the Jews a convenient source of revenue. In 1290 Edward I adopted the more summary method of expelling all Jews from England and confiscating their lands and houses. A considerable number of tenements occupied by them in Cambridge were acquired by religious houses.

In the disputes between the Town and the University the alleged grievances were not all on the part of the former. An item in the scholars' indictment of the borough authorities was their neglect of sanitary precautions—in particular, their failure to cleanse the King's Ditch. As the Ditch was the King's, perhaps the Corporation held the view that its purgation was the King's business. The King passed on the duty to the Mayor and bailiffs, and that they neglected it is clear, since townsmen themselves complained of encroachments, obstructions and nuisances caused by dwellers in the neighbourhood of the Ditch. In 1330 the University presented a petition to Parliament complaining, among other matters, that the mayor and bailiffs did not keep the streets free from filth and dirt, and especially that they did not scour the Ditch. As happens in similar cases nowadays, ' nothing was done.' On July 14, 1348, King Edward III, under menace of a great calamity, awaked to the responsibilities of the Crown in the matter, and issued a commission to enquire into the condition of the Ditch, and ascertain who was bound to cleanse it. Still nothing effectual seems to have resulted, for once more, about the year 1351, the University petitioned Parliament that the townsmen should be compelled to cleanse the streets, then noxious to inhabitants and passers-by.

But before this second petition the disaster, present when the King issued his commission in 1348, had fallen on Cambridge. The Black Death, which in the universality of its devastation far outwent any subsequent visitation of plague, was brought to England in the autumn of 1348. Warnings of its ravages beyond sea in the summer of that year had reached the country, and sporadic measures had been taken to counter its invasion. It reached the Eastern counties in the spring of 1349, and in no part of the kingdom were its horrors more appalling. In Norwich it is estimated that 57,000 inhabitants were carried off out of an estimated population of 70,000 ; in Yarmouth 7000 died. In Cambridgeshire the disease was at its height from April to June, 1349. Of the 142 benefices in the diocese of Ely 97 were vacated in the course of the year ; in 1348 the number was only seven. At Cambridge, the Mayor, Robert Brigham, and three successive Masters of the Hospital of St John died. Sixteen of the forty scholars of King's Hall, which adjoined the Hospital, died between April and August. In a document, dated 1366 and addressed to the Bishop, the Prior and Convent of Ely give their consent to a proposal of the Bishop to unite the parishes of St Giles and All Saints by the Castle. It states that the parishioners of the latter parish are most of them dead of the pestilence, and adds that the bones of the dead in the churchyard are exposed to wild beasts. In September, 1349, the Bishop's Vicar addressed a letter to the vicar of All Saints in the Jewry in which, on the ground that the parishioners had been so swept away by the plague that the offerings of the church did not suffice for the necessaries of food and clothing, he authorises him to have for two years an anniversary mass for his support. Similar permission was given to the vicar of St John's in Milne Street.[1]

The ruin of the town was completed by the devastation of the shire of which it was the capital. Manor rolls show that lands were uncultivated, houses and cottages vacant and rents unpaid. One symptom is to be noted, as premonitory of a revolution in the agricultural system. The personal services which used to be rendered by tenants had to be commuted for a payment in money. The bitterness of the contrast between the misery and subjection of the Town and the relatively prosperous state of the University undoubtedly accentuated the violence of the outbreak at Cambridge, which attended the Peasants' Rising of 1381. Though the Rising was far too general and concerted throughout England to be attributed to merely local grievances, the commonalty of the town seized the opportunity of paying off some old reckonings with their enemies, the clerks. In 1278, when the burgesses complained to Edward I of the encroachments of the University, no colleges were in existence, and the University itself hardly owned a rood of ground within the borough limits. In the century which followed eight colleges had arisen, and they owned a large amount of property in the town. The latest foundation, that of Corpus Christi, especially invited the animosity of the townsmen. Founded by townsmen

---

[1] Gaskin, *The Great Pestilence*, 133–135.

Mackenzie.   J. Le Keux.

CAMBRIDGE FROM THE CASTLE HILL, IN 1842

and for their religious benefit, they deemed it to have betrayed its trust by allying itself with the University. It owned more property in the borough than any then existing college, and it exacted a particularly invidious tax, called *candle rents, i.e.* rents originally charged on town houses for the purpose of supplying lights for the services of the Gilds, but afterwards diverted to the ordinary purposes of a University college. Its special patron was John of Gaunt, the most detested man in England. It had farm property in Grantchester, and it is noteworthy that the leaders of the mob at Cambridge came from that village.

The insurrection, which began with the meeting of the armed peasants at Blackheath on June 12, speedily extended itself to the Eastern Counties. On Saturday, June 15, the bailiffs and commonalty of Cambridge, by the advice and with the consent of the Mayor, met together and went to Shingay Hospital, where they joined another party of rioters and destroyed the house of a landowner, named Thomas Hasilden, drove away his horses, sheep and pigs, and carried off his goods and chattels. They chose as their leaders two brothers, James and Thomas of Grantchester, and at 10 o'clock the same night assembled at the Tolbooth and proceeded to the house of one of the University bedels, William Wygmer, which they destroyed. Afterwards they went to Corpus Christi College, broke open the scholars' chambers and took away all the charters, writings and effects of the college. At St Mary's church they rifled the University chest and burnt all the bulls, muniments and charters contained in it.

Next day, Sunday, they again assembled in great routs and, marching out of the town, brought back with them the rioters of the county. Thereupon the mayor, bailiffs and commonalty compelled the University to execute deeds renouncing all their privileges and submitting themselves to be governed by the law of the land and the ancient custom of the borough.

They also compelled the masters and scholars by menace of death to deliver up their charters, statutes and evidences and burnt them in the market place, amidst the rejoicings of the populace. An old woman, named Margaret Starre, gathering the ashes of the burning documents, scattered them in the air, exclaiming 'Away with the skill of the clerks, away with it.'

On Monday, June 17, the populace assembled in great numbers on Midsummer Common and repaired to the Priory at Barnwell, where they broke down the Prior's close, carried away a great number of trees, 'as if,' says Fuller, 'they bare such hatred to all wood, they would not leave any to make gallows for thieves and murderers,' and made other great affrays.[1]

Hearing of these disorders the bishop of Norwich, Henry le Spencer, who was then at his house of Burley, near Oakham, marched to Cambridge with a small troop of lances and archers, attacked the rebels, killed some and captured others. The rebels of Norfolk and Suffolk he sent home under oath that they would not again take arms against the King. Between July 16 and Oct. 23 the King issued a series of commissions to enquire into the misdemeanours committed and to compel guilty parties to make restitution or compensation.

In the Parliament which began at Westminster in the following November, on the complaint of the University, the Mayor and bailiffs were summoned by writ to appear and answer for the deeds forcibly

---

[1] The attack on the property of the Barnwell canons was the outcome of the popular grievance about 'enclosure' of common lands. After the suppression of the rising the Prior presented a bill of trespass against the Mayor. It was therein alleged that the Mayor 'and his commons' with force and arms broke the close of the Prior and Convent, to wit, walls, palings and hays, and cut down and carried off the trees growing there to the value of £400, and broke the palings and gates of the Watergate and carried off the gates and other things, to wit, fish, sedge, turf and other things, to the damage of the Prior and Convent to the amount of £2000. The Mayor pleaded that whatever had been done was done by a mob which threatened him with decapitation, and he further alleged that for time beyond memory the burgesses and commons had possessed right of pasture for their beasts on Estenhale common, adjoining the Priory, which had been wrongfully enclosed by the Prior with fences and hedges. Possibly the Mayor was inaccurate in fact; certainly the Prior's claim for damages was preposterous in amount. (Maitland, *Township and Borough*, 192.)

obtained from the University. These were now delivered up and, having been read to the Parliament, were ordered to be cancelled and made void. Then the University exhibited a bill setting forth in detail the excesses and acts of violence of which the Mayor, bailiffs and burgesses had been guilty. The accused persons stated that the insurrection was confined to the lower orders of the town and the traitors from Kent, Essex and Hertford, who came to the town in prodigious numbers; that the Mayor, bailiffs and other gentlemen and persons of consequence had taken no part in the outrages, and had done their best to restore peace and order; and that all the delinquents who had been apprehended had been put to death, and the rest had fled the country. To this it was replied that the Mayor and bailiffs were always present with the rioters, agreeing with what they did.

The King, by assent of the prelates and lords of Parliament, thereupon caused the franchises of the Town to be seized into his hands as forfeited. But in the following year he restored to the Town all its liberties, except the assize of bread, wine and ale, and the survey of weights and measures, together with fines and amerciaments thence arising, which were assigned to the Chancellor and scholars. At the same time four marks were added to the 101 hitherto paid as the farm of the town.

CHAPTER X.

The Fifteenth Century

THE space which is devoted in Cooper's *Annals* to the records of Cambridge in the fifteenth century is equal to that occupied by all preceding centuries. The accounts of the Town Treasurers begin, as a connected series, with the reign of Henry VI, and contain some interesting information on municipal matters. But for the space of nearly a century which intervenes between the death of the second Richard in Pomfret Castle and the finding of the crown of the third of that name on Bosworth Field, there is nothing in them of national concern. The shire, having no great landlord who was interested in dynastic concerns, was comfortably removed from the internecine warfare of the rival Roses. But, on the whole, the annals of the time convey the sense that Cambridge shared in the general depression of the nation resulting from pestilence, foreign war and civil unrest.

The quarrels between Town and Gown persisted with the old bitterness, but throughout the period the University more than maintained its suzerainty, and began to oust the burghers from their very homes and trade centres. Henry VI, by his foundation of King's College, made a vast clearance in the middle of the town, and as his plans for the building of the Great Court for centuries took no effect, the bleating of sheep there succeeded to the hum of human activity. The important thoroughfare of Milne Street was enclosed in the greater part of its course, as well as the whole of Pyrones Lane and Strawy Lane, which led from Milne Street to the river bank, In recompense of the loss of access to the river by the closed lanes the King, indeed, granted the Town some ground whereon a new passage was made, which still exists as Garret Hostel

Lane. But no new hithe was established there, and
from the Bridge to the Mills the town was effectually
divorced from the river trade, which had been a main
source of its prosperity. With Milne Street the church
and parish of St John disappeared, as well as an inn,
the Boar's Head, a hithe called Salthithe and a multitude of private houses and tenements. A considerable
part of the town pasture was annexed to the College,
together with many houses bordering the High Street.

The poverty of the town during the greater part of
the fifteenth century is patent. In 1385 more than a
hundred tenements, with all that they contained, were
consumed by accidental fires. Many people quitted
the town, and in consequence the burgesses, in 1402,
represented to the King that they were unable to pay
the customary farm of the town. Again, in 1446, they
complained that houses formerly occupied by craftsmen,
were now inhabited by scholars, and were not chargeable
for the town relief; that the clearance made for the
King's College had left a large quarter untenanted;
and that in consequence craftsmen were quitting the
town, which was thereby utterly impoverished.

The church architecture of Cambridge may be cited
as evidence that the fifteenth century was on the whole
a time of stagnation. Many of the churches, viewed
externally, present the aspect of buildings of that
century, but this is due to the character of their aisles.
Aisles were added, about this time, to the churches of
St Botolph, St Clement and St Edward, and the
transepts to Holy Trinity. But as one motive in
building them was to provide side chapels, it does not
follow that the parishes had increased in population,
and it has to be remembered that the parishes of St
John in Milne Street and All Saints next the Castle
disappeared in the century between 1350 and 1450,
and the parishioners were transferred to other parishes.
Great St Mary's was entirely rebuilt in the last quarter
of the fifteenth century, but it took thirty years to

complete the nave, and the tower was not finished until
1608. The Guildhall, or Tolbooth, was built in 1386,
but it was diminutive in size and unpretending in
architecture.

Pestilence, no doubt, played its part in arresting the
growth of the population at Cambridge, as elsewhere.
After the great outbreak of 1349 there was a constant
recurrence of sick seasons. In 1389 there was 'a sad
mortality in the Town and University, proceeding
from the infection of the air, and that caused from the
unclean keeping of the streets.' In 1447 Henry VI
had intended in person to lay the first stone of King's
Chapel, but 'for the aier and the Pestilence that hath
long regned in our said Universite we come not at this
time,' and, as the same prudential reason does not
apply to relations, 'we send thidder our Cousin the
Marquess of Suffolk.' In 1485 a disease, new, or newly
named, called 'the sweat,' visited the town, and again
between 1491 and 1495. The Lady Margaret in
her will provided that her manor house at Malton
should be built for the scholars of Christ's College
'to resort thidder and there to tarye in tyme of siknes
at Cambrige.' For the like purpose the students of
Physwick's Hostel had a place of retirement at
Titchwell in Norfolk.

Doubtless there had been visitations at Cambridge
before 1348, but the town annals are silent respecting
them. Even in later times, when the chronicles are
fuller, there is the barest mention of them. Plague
was regarded so much as an ordinary event that it
required less comment than the appearance of a comet.
But it may be surmised that the conditions of town life
after 1348 made the recurrence of the disease more
frequent and its devastation more deadly than in the
earlier times, and especially so at Cambridge. The
gathering of students from all parts of the British Isles
must have rendered the town particularly open to
infection. The great fair at Sturbridge, falling at an

unhealthy season of the year, must have been still more potent in attracting disease, and for the thousands who encamped on Sturbridge Common we may feel sure that no sanitary provision of an adequate kind was attempted. The only thing to be done—and it was constantly done—was to inhibit the holding of the fair in pestilence years; and for the same reason the University dispensed its scholars from residence and lectures in not fewer than fifteen years of the sixteenth century. At a time when the Great Fen reached almost to the skirts of the town and marshes were spread along the upper branches of the river, ague, the 'tertian' or 'quartan' fever so familiar to our ancestors, was endemic and, if not in itself a destroyer, was the vaunt-courier of epidemic disease.

Medieval Cambridge had every feature, physical and artificial, which should encourage disease. Though it contained open spaces which preserved for it some of the aspect of an agricultural settlement, its streets were narrow and the houses in them were perhaps more closely packed then than now. In 1584 the Privy Council called the attention of the Vice-Chancellor and Mayor to the danger of plague ' by reason that so many poor people are so narrowly and unwholesomely thrust and thronged together in divers places': but no action seems to have come of the admonition. Everywhere the ground was scored with open ditches —some of them very ancient—but the elevation of the greater part of the town above the river was so slight and the fall of the river so insignificant that the water which they contained was virtually stagnant, and the gutters which were supposed to drain the streets were rather an additional source of impurity. The King's Ditch was the Cloaca Maxima of Cambridge, and, as Fuller says, what was made for the fortifying became the annoying of the town. Within twelve months of the time when it was made, or re-made, by Henry III we find the King enacting that it should

F

be kept open, as of old time it used, so that filth might run off. But the filth did not run off, and the order had to be constantly repeated. Town and University perpetually complain of the ' seges or privies ' which either body suffers to be placed over it ; and the other ' Common Ditches ' were in the like evil case.

Except on the slope of the Castle Hill, where the Canons of St Giles in their first location found a lack of ' living springs,' water is to be found everywhere and easily under the surface of the soil. Until 1853, when the Waterworks Company was started, and when water was brought from the chalk-hills of Cherry-hinton, Cambridge was perfectly satisfied with its indigenous Abanas and Pharpars, however small their healthful and cleansing properties. Until the last quarter of the nineteenth century half the lodging-houses licensed by the University were supplied from pumps. The sources were always shallow and the soil was saturated with the pollutions incidental to its long occupation by an urban population. The anti-quity of pumps and their persistence in a given place is extraordinary. In his plan of Cambridge, drawn in 1594. Hamond, with his accustomed fidelity, marks a pump-handle projecting from the wall which bounds Holy Trinity churchyard. In his view of Trinity Church, dated 1816, Ackerman shows a pump in exactly the same position, with a woman filling her pail thereat, and the earth of the adjoining churchyard is piled high above the street level. Wiser than their lay neighbours, the Franciscan friars, in 1434, made themselves an aqueduct to bring water to their house from a spring near the Observatory, where the Conduit house stands to this day.[1] In 1441 the scholars of

---

[1] In 1350, just after the Black Death, the Mayor and commonalty granted to the Carmelite Friars a well of water outside the town, called Hoker's well, and land, ten by ten feet in circuit, about it, with leave to enclose it with a wall, and to make an underground aqueduct from the well to their manse, which was in Milne Street. (*Patent Rolls.*) The well in question was somewhere in the Western Field (*Priory of St Radegund*, charter 330). It seems to have taken its name from a certain Osmund Hoccere, who owned land at Cambridge in the tenth century. (*Liber Eliensis*, 131.)

King's Hall obtained leave to make a 'quill,' or pipe, from this aqueduct to supply their outer court, as it still supplies the fountain in the Great Court of Trinity. A conduit in the middle of the court was a feature in King Henry's VI's abortive plan of King's College; but the College only acquired its fountain in 1879. There was also a 'fountain' in the Market place in the fifteenth century—evidently a well, for water was not brought by a conduit to the Market until the seventeenth century. The so-called Hobson's conduit was built in 1624. Well Lane, or Pump Lane, which ran north and south at the eastern end of Great St Mary's church, took its name from another pump which stood in the middle of the lane.

For the paving of the streets the Mayor and bailiffs from time to time were empowered by the King to take tolls on certain articles of merchandise brought into the town. Complaints were made that the money so received was misapplied by individuals to their own use, and the University had frequent cause to draw the King's attention to the neglect of the town authorities in the matter. As every householder, 'according to the custom of the town,' was compelled to pave before his tenement the authorities seem to have regarded their duties as sufficiently discharged when they had received the paving toll, and they eased their consciences by devolving their responsibilities on charitable and religious persons. In 1290 the Chancellor of the University paved the town, and had license to raise a toll for six years for the purpose. A bishop of Ely, in 1399, granted indulgence to such persons as should contribute to the repair of the Trumpington road: and in the same year, the bridges and road between Cambridge and Newnham being in a dangerous state of disrepair, John Jaye, the hermit of the Small Bridges chapel, was authorised by the King to take customs of articles brought for sale along that road, to be applied to its reparation. Stone for that purpose was unprocurable, and an order of the Corporation, in 1428, licensed the hermit of that day to use the willows growing on either side of the causeway for the repair and maintenance of 'the slippery and dangerous way near the aforesaid bridges and causeway.' Such being the 'metal' employed, we may the better understand an ordinance of 1402 forbidding carriers to use wheels of iron, or shod with iron. In 1477 we hear of stones being brought 'in vessels called keeles' to mend the pavements of the town.

All imaginable filth was allowed to lie in the streets and Market-place. Foul Lane, now Trinity Lane, amply justified its name. In 1393 it was stated that many masters and scholars passing through that street fell sick owing to its abominable stench. An order of 1402, intended to improve sanitation, directed that no one should allow dung and filth to be left in the Market-place or elsewhere, unless it were removed within seven days. By a compact between the Town and University, in 1503, it was covenanted that the Corporation, *once in three years*, should cleanse the 'common sege' of the town.

In the latter half of the fifteenth century certain indications of reviving prosperity begin to show themselves in the benefactions of well-to-do burghers for charitable purposes. The first endowment of the kind falls within the preceding century. In 1361 Henry de Tangmer founded the Hospital of St Anthony and St Eligius, which was situated at the angle of Trumpington Street and Lensfield Road, and gave to this suburb the name of Spital End. In 1459 another burgher, Richard Andrewe, or Spycer, bequeathed to the Town a sum of eighty marks, to be deposited in a hutch, or chest, from which townsmen, on giving pledges, might borrow sums not exceeding 26s. 8d. The hutch still exists and is used to contain muniments of the Corporation. In 1469 the first almshouses in the town were built and endowed by Thomas

Jackenett. They were for four poor men or women, and adjoined the west end of Great St Mary's church. They have been transferred to King Street.

Of the general conditions of trade in the fifteenth century there is provokingly small witness in the town annals. None but free burgesses were entitled to set up in business at Cambridge. If a stranger brought merchandise to the market he had to pay toll at the Tolbooth there; if to the Fair, at another Tolbooth at Sturbridge. Only burgesses could own booths at Sturbridge Fair: if they let them to 'foreigners' one-third of the sum for which they were let was to be paid to the Mayor and bailiffs. A burgess might claim the privilege of freedom for one son; the fine was 6s. 8d., but if the father were dead when the son was admitted, it was reduced to 3s. 4d. A 'foreigner' might obtain freedom for a son or apprentice by a payment, the amount of which was determined by two burgesses assigned for the purpose by the Corporation. An apprentice was required to serve for seven years before he could be qualified for the freedom; the master must bring him to the Tolbooth before the end of his term and pay the fine for him. On payment of a fine of 3s. 4d. a man might acquire freedom by marriage with a woman who was possessed of land in the borough or of booths in the Fair. It looks as though the possession of freehold within the borough was an essential condition of freedom, as residence in the borough undoubtedly was. Exactly what went to the making of burghership we cannot say. Everybody in the fifteenth century assumed that everybody knew who were burgesses, what were their qualifications and what their privileges; custom made definition needless. Within the wide limits of custom there was ample room for the abuses of non-resident and honorary freemen, which were the scandal of the seventeenth and eighteenth centuries.

Chapter XI.

The Reformation

In the reign of Henry VIII the Reformation overcasts all other events at Cambridge, as elsewhere. Books were the spawn of the Reformation, and it is worth enquiring what part Cambridge took in the production of them.

Bookselling with its related trades was a Cambridge industry as old as the University itself. In the reign of Edward I we find householders with significant names such as Lominor (the illuminator) and Parchiminere or Parmenter (dealer in parchment). In the fifteenth century the University employed certain 'stationaries,' who were not students but 'privileged persons.' It was the practice of those days for students to deposit with the proctors 'cautions,' or pledges that they would proceed to their exercises and degrees in due course. The cautions consisted usually of books, and it was the stationaries' business to value them, or sell them if unredeemed. In 1480 the University passed a Grace that no book written or printed on paper should be accepted as a pledge; but the prohibition was sometimes disregarded. A paper mill existed at Cambridge in 1557, and perhaps earlier: it stood on the stream which crosses the Newmarket road, opposite the Globe Inn. The University claimed that all booksellers, bookbinders and stationers, living within its precincts, were subject to its jurisdiction, and required that they should have its license, and should enter into bond that they would supply the students with books at reasonable prices. The University control did not extend to the fairs, and it is likely that the trade in books at Sturbridge was important from early times. Towards the end of the seventeenth century the booksellers occupied a part of Cooks' Row at the Fair, and auctions of books were held there on a very extensive scale and advertised in the London Gazette.[1]

Booksellers (*bibliopolae*) established themselves in Cambridge very soon after Caxton settled at Westminster and produced the first book printed in England (1477). In a list (1503) of scholars' servants enjoying the privileges of the University occurs the name of ' Garreit, stacioner.' This was Garret, or Gerard, Godfrey, well known as the friend of Erasmus and of Ascham. He was a churchwarden of Great St Mary's, and died in 1539. Specimens of his binding, bearing his initials, G.G., are to be found in many Cambridge libraries. Writing in 1525 to his friend, Robert Aldrich of King's College, Erasmus sends greeting to Gerard and to two other Cambridge booksellers, Nicholas and John Siburg. John Siburg, or Siberch, otherwise known as John Lair de Siberch, was the first Cambridge printer, and occupied a house called Arma Regia, opposite St Michael's church. Several books came from his press in 1521 and 1522. He was a member of the University, described as *bibliopola* and ' an alien priest.' In 1520 he was printing at Cologne. It is noteworthy that the printers and sellers of books at Cambridge in the earlier part of the sixteenth century were mostly foreigners.[2] In fact the University in a petition addressed to Cardinal Wolsey, in 1524, expressed a desire that its booksellers should be aliens, on the ground that their books were cheaper and that they could better procure them from foreign dealers.

---

[1] Mayor, *Cambridge Under Queen Anne*, 249.

[2] Nicholas Spierinck, appointed stationer in 1534, Nicholas Pylgrym, in 1539, and Peter Shers, in 1545, were all foreigners: all of them were parishioners of Great St Mary's. An interesting account of Cambridge book trade from the earliest times to the present day is given in G. J. Gray's *Cambridge Bookselling* (1925).

After the disappearance of Siberch's press no books were printed at Cambridge until 1584. Though the University appointed John Kingston its printer in 1577, objection was raised to the appointment by Lord Burghley on the ground that it prejudiced the printers licensed by the Queen. A similar objection was raised in 1583 to the appointment of Thomas Thomas, a Fellow of King's College, and his press was seized and removed by the Company of Stationers, but it was restored in the following year: however, by a decree of the Star Chamber the University was limited to one press and one apprentice at most. Between 1584 and 1588, when Thomas died, seventeen books were issued by him. His printing house was in the Regent Walk, a street opposite the west door of Great St Mary's church and leading to the Schools. The University printers occupied the same or adjoining premises until Thomas Buck, about 1632, removed his press to the old house of the Austin Friars in Free School Lane.

Throughout the sixteenth century the press was regarded with great suspicion by the Government, which had as keen a scent for schismatical literature after the Reformation as for heresy before it. After 1554 all booksellers and books had to be licensed by the Stationers' Company. When, in 1529, the University presented its petition to Wolsey that it should be allowed three booksellers, the suppression of error was made the ground of the request. The pole of authorised belief had varied surprisingly in 1534, when the three booksellers were appointed; for among them was Sygar Nicholson. In 1529 he had been charged with having in his house the works of Luther and other prohibited books. He was thrown into prison and compelled to abjure, and the incriminated books were burnt. When John Hullier of King's College was burnt on Jesus Green Sygar gave him gunpowder to end his suffering (1556).

Nothing in the fifteenth century annals of Cambridge foreboded the religious tornado which in England fell in fullest force on the Eastern counties. If Lollardy existed before then it was but as smoking flax. In 1457 Bishop Gray of Ely, when required by the Archbishop of Canterbury to make inquisition in his diocese for heretical books, made reply that none were to be found; and at a rather earlier date John Lydgate for the University was bold to pronounce that 'of heresie Cambridge bare never blame.' As a popular movement the Reformation came with printed books, and books, as has been shown, were imported by foreigners. An old distich said

> Hops, Reformation, bays and beer
> Came into England all in one year.

The concatenation was not fortuitous. The cultivation of hops was introduced into the Eastern counties from the Netherlands about the end of the fifteenth century, and in Erasmus' day a Dutch beer-brewer, Francis van Hoorn, had established a business at Cambridge, between the river and Magdalene College, and in this he was succeeded by Sygar Nicholson. The vulgar association of beer and Bible had perhaps better warrant four hundred years ago than to-day. It is worth remarking that in the reign of Edward VI the White Horse Inn, celebrated as the meeting-place of the first Cambridge Reformers, was occupied by Emanuel Tremellius, originally an Italian Jew, who lectured in the University on Hebrew and was noted as an earnest Protestant. Possibly his predecessor in the tenancy of the inn was also a favourer of the Reformed teaching and in sympathy with the 'Germans' who frequented his house.[1]

The English Reformation, on its scholarly side, may be called a Cambridge movement. It had its

---

[1] Baize (bays) was one of the staple manufactures of Norwich. In the sixteenth century four thousand natives of the Netherlands were settled in the city, which was a hot-bed of Reformation. The first book printed in Norwich was produced in 1570 by one of these settlers.

seeds in the teaching of Erasmus, who was resident in the University from 1509 to 1513, and its first apostles reflected the light of the Cambridge schools. It is a noteworthy matter that a large proportion of them were of Norfolk birth and belonged to the Norfolk colleges, Gonvile Hall and Trinity Hall. In the Marian reaction the number of the Protestant martyrs in Norwich diocese was forty-six—more than in any diocese except London and Canterbury. It might be surmised that the popular influences which were at work in Norfolk extended to the neighbour and kindred county of Cambridge. If it were so we have little evidence of the fact. The leaven of Lutheranism worked most strongly among the industrial population of large centres, such as Norwich, Yarmouth and Lynn; but, apart from the University, Cambridge ranked with minor towns, and its connections with foreign trade were unimportant. The town produced no martyrs and no missionaries. Of its attitude to the new doctrines little is to be gathered from the local annals.

Nevertheless the first open challenge to the Roman hierarchy came not from the University schools or pulpit, but was addressed to a town audience in a parish church. On Christmas Eve, 1525, Dr Barnes preached in the church of St Edward, which adjoined the house of the Austin friars, of which he was prior. In his sermon he indulged in bitter invectives against the whole priestly order, not sparing the all-powerful Wolsey himself. The parish contained the Butchers' Row, and the preacher adapted his address to the calling of his audience, not without a sidelong reference to the story that the Cardinal was a butcher's son. The pastoral staff, said he, was more like to knock swine on the head than to take sheep: 'a foolish thing,' said Bishop Fisher, 'to preach before all the butchers of Cambridge.' With what measure of agreement the Cambridge tradesmen listened to the orator we cannot say: but we may guess that plain speech on the corruptions of the Church found attentive listeners among them, for at another Christmas season, four years later, in the same church, Latymer preached his two famous sermons 'On the Card.'

A visitor to Cambridge at the end of the fifteenth century would have taken note that it contained more than the usual number of houses of religion. Compared with Ely or Bury none of them would appear to be of more than ordinary consequence, but in the size and character of their buildings and the extent of their grounds they far surpassed anything which the colleges had yet to show. The parish churches, without exception, were small and unpretentious, and important secular buildings or private houses hardly existed. Only a wealthy community could command the stone and timber which Nature denies to the environs of Cambridge.

For some half-century before the General Dissolution the conclusion had been forced on the authorities of the Church that the monastic establishments generally had ceased to be an active influence in popular religion and had forfeited the esteem of the nation. Reforming bishops such as Wolsey, Fox, Fisher and Alcock, saw that the security of the Church lay in an alliance with the Universities. To this cause, more than to the corruption which was laid to their charge, must be attributed the conversion of the old foundations of St Radegund's Nunnery and the Hospital of St John into the colleges of Jesus and St John, and, no doubt, the Reformation only precipitated an event which would have followed without its momentum. Even in the religious orders there was a section which looked not unkindly on the reformed doctrines. Among the friars, who had always associated themselves with the liberal studies of the University, the progressive tendency was especially noticeable. Robert Barnes, Prior of the Augustinians, was the protagonist of the Reform movement and presided at the discussions of

the 'Germans' at the White Horse Inn. Miles
Coverdale and William Paynell of the same house were
active as his lieutenants. Though Cranmer, writing
to Cromwell, remarks of Oliver, Prior of the Dominicans, that he was 'of small learning, sinister behaviour
and ill qualities,' he adds that there were in the same
house men of good study, living, learning and
judgment. Among the brethren of either house
who signed the surrender were several who attained
high station in the Reformed Church.

Of the religious houses Barnwell Priory was the
oldest and by far the wealthiest. Its annual revenues
were rated at £256—a sum only exceeded by four
colleges, King's, St John's, Christ's, and Queens'.
The Canons had shown small desire to avail themselves
of the advantages of University education, and probably
were deaf to the voices of reform. Their Prior, Nicholas
Smith, was compelled to resign in 1534, and was allowed
a pension of £20. His successor, John Badcock, was
evidently put in as a man known to be amenable to
the King's will; he was a member of the University,
took a divinity degree in 1559, and after the dissolution
resided in Jesus College, and was vicar of St Andrew's,
Barnwell. He received a pension of £6. The surrender of the house, dated November 8, 1538, was
subscribed by the Prior and six Canons. The Priory
had parted with its interest in Midsummer Fair to the
Town in 1506.

The Friars' houses were dissolved about the same time
as Barnwell Priory. As the Mendicant orders were
supposed to subsist on alms and had no estates beyond
their conventual sites and buildings we have no information about their income. The letting value of the
large area occupied by the Franciscans was stated as
only £4 6s. 8d. Their house was surrendered to the
Crown by the Warden, William White, the Vice-
Warden and twenty-two brethren. The great hall
of this body had been used by the University for its

THE OLD HOUSES, KING'S PARADE

85

annual Commencement ceremonies, and in 1539 the University petitioned for a grant of the house and site. The King had other designs and bestowed them on the College, Trinity, which he was then proposing to erect. The buildings were already ' defaced ' in 1546, and the site remained vacant until the College sold it to the executors of the Countess of Sussex for the establishment of Sidney Sussex College. Before that time, in 1576, the Corporation had designed to procure the site from Trinity College for a hospital for the poor of the town.

The surrender of the house of the Dominicans was signed by the Prior and fifteen brethren. In this house there was ' an Ymage of ower Lady,' which was the resort of many pilgrims, especially at the time of Sturbridge Fair. The site was leased to a townsman, and at one time it was proposed to grant it to St Nicholas' Hostel. Ultimately it was acquired by Sir Walter Mildmay for his foundation of Emmanuel College.

On September 6 the Carmelites surrendered their house to the King. The deed of surrender was signed by the Prior, Clement Hubberd, *alias* Thorpe, and five brethren. Hubberd had only become Prior since August 8 preceding, on which day George Legate, Prior, and two brethren, ' gladly, freely and willingly ' surrendered their house to the President and Fellows of Queens' College. The King treated the earlier surrender as void, but sold the materials of the house to the College for £20. The site was divided between King's College and Queens' College. An inventory of the moveable goods of the friars shows that they were a poor community.

Of the Austin friars only the Prior and three brethren witnessed the deed of surrender. The house and grounds were purchased in 1545 by Dr Hatcher, Vice-Chancellor of the University in 1579, who devised them in his will, dated 1584, to the University to be employed as a house for students; but this part of the will never took effect. Early in the seventeenth century part of the building, seemingly the old refectory, was occupied by Thomas Buck as a printing house. This part, which faced Peas Hill, was in existence in 1770, and had large gates resembling those of a college. The extensive grounds passed into the hands of Stephen Perse, and on a part of them the Perse Grammar School and Almshouses were built. Other parts were purchased by Dr Walker in 1760 to serve as the University Botanic Garden.[1]

There is no record of the surrender of the house of the White, or Gilbertine, Canons in Trumpington Street. The establishment was poor and its revenue was reckoned at little more than £14.

An Act of Parliament of 1545 authorised the confiscation of gild property. Unfortunately there is no record of the gilds then in existence at Cambridge. The traces of craft gilds are scanty. The shearers in Shearers' Row and the woolcombers, who had a procession on St Blaise's day, possibly had their gilds, and the skinners formed one in honour of St Katherine, but it was not limited to their craft. Eight religious gilds were in existence in 1389; but the two most important—those of St Mary and Corpus Christi, which combined to found Corpus Christi College— lapsed in the reign of Richard II, probably in consequence of the rising in 1381, when the College was an object of popular hostility. In 1483 the gild of St Katherine in St Andrew's church had its hall where the members dined, and it still survived in 1500. About the latter year we hear of two gilds in Great St Mary's church. The churchwardens

---

[1] Dr Hatcher's house was immensely large. An inventory made at the time of his death, in 1587, mentions twenty-seven rooms, besides outhouses. The 'great parlour,' probably the refectory of the Friars, was 70 yards long, and other rooms were scarcely less spacious; the 'great chamber' had an oriel window twelve feet broad (Dr W. M. Palmer in C.A.S. *Communications* xv. 240–242). In 1783 the house had become ruinous, and was sold with the site by the University to Mr John Mortlock for £150.

of the same church were made a body corporate in 1535.[1]

In 1547 an Act was passed for suppressing chantries and free chapels. In 1544 the Bishop and Chapter of Ely, perhaps with prescience of this event, leased the chapel at Sturbridge with all its revenues from farms or booths in the fair, valued at £10 10s., to the Corporation for sixty years, but after the suppression the Corporation held the lease of the King. The dissolved chantries were in the churches of St Clement, St Sepulchre, Little St Mary, and Great St Mary.

On the death of Edward VI a momentary spark from London alighted at Cambridge, but failed to produce a conflagration. The Council, under the influence of the Duke of Northumberland, proclaimed the Lady Jane Grey as Queen on July 10, 1553, and took steps to arrest the Lady Mary. She was then at Hunsdon, in Hertfordshire, but on hearing of the King's death she came to Sawston, where she was received by Sir John Huddleston, and then proceeded to Framlingham, in Suffolk, where her adherents raised for her a great force. The Council therefore ordered the despatch towards Cambridge of an army of 8000 foot and 2000 horse. The Duke, who was in personal command of this force, reached Cambridge on July 15, and was waited on by the leaders of the Protestant party in the University, and next day, being Sunday, at his request the Vice-Chancellor, Dr Sandys, preached a sermon in the interests of the succession of the Lady Jane Grey. But the Duke, whose unscrupulous ambition made him the most hated man in England, failed to obtain the reinforcements promised by the Council, and his own men deserted him. On July 19 Mary was proclaimed Queen by

---

[1] For earlier gilds, most of which were extinct in 1545, see p. 39. Craft gilds being scarcely known at Cambridge, it is a little remarkable that the gild of the Annunciation in Great St Mary's excluded from its membership all parsons and all bakers. The exclusion of ecclesiastics is intelligible, and the gild of the Assumption in Trinity Church applied the same rule to them; but what personal antipathies underlie the disqualification of bakers?

the Council in London. Next day, about five in the
evening, the Duke, 'with such other of the nobilitie
as were in his company, came to the market cross of
the town, and, calling for an Herault, himself proclaimed the Queen Mary, and among others he threwe
uppe his owne cappe, and so laughed that the tears
ran down his cheeks for grief.' Within an hour of the
proclamation a pursuivant arrived with instructions
that he should notify that the Duke, if he did not submit
himself to Queen Mary, should be held a traitor.
Shortly afterwards the Duke was arrested in King's
College by Roger Slegge, who afterwards was an
alderman of the town. He showed contemptible
cowardice, and when taken to London, avowed himself
a Catholic and even heard Mass on the scaffold: but
his recantation availed him nothing.

Only one martyr suffered at Cambridge in the days
of Marian persecution. He was John Hullier, formerly
a scholar and Conduct of King's College, but at the
time of his arrest a preacher at Lynn. Thence he was
brought to Cambridge and lodged first in the Castle,
afterwards in the Tolbooth prison. He suffered on
Jesus Green on Maundy Thursday, 1556. Whatever
may have been the indifference of the townspeople at
the first stirring of the religious revolution their feelings
at his death were manifested in a tempest of sympathy
for him and abhorrence of the deed. 'His flesh being
consumed, his bones stood upright, even as if they had
been alive. Of the people some took what they could
get of him, as pieces of bones. One had his heart, the
which was distributed as far as it would go: one took the
scalp and looked for the tongue, but it was consumed,
except the very root.'

Next year there came to Cambridge the Visitors of
the University, delegated by Cardinal Pole. With
their pompous peregrination of the Colleges and high-
handed treatment of lapsed University officials the
Town had no concern. One crowning act of their

G

barbarity was the exhumation of the bodies of the German Reformers, Paul Fagius and Martin Bucer, who had died at Cambridge during the late King's reign, and were buried, the one in St Michael's church, the other in Great St Mary's. Their remains, enclosed in chests and chained to stakes, were burnt on a market day in the Market Place, after which the churches in which they had been buried were ceremoniously ' reconciled.' All, and more than all, the structure that the Visitors had re-erected was swept away by another Commission appointed two years later by Elizabeth.

CHAPTER XII.

The Poor and the Commons

In continuing the story of the religious revolution at
Cambridge down to the accession of Elizabeth we have
overstepped an event in the reign of Edward VI which
had something more than local significance and, at
the time, perhaps claimed quite as much attention as
the warfare of the creeds. In 1549 there was 'the
insurrection' at Cambridge, which coincided with the
rising in Norfolk under Ket.

In the middle of the sixteenth century the town had
all the aspect of an agricultural community. It was
the nucleus of a cultivated area comprising some five
square miles. In one direction the town Fields reached
from the bounds of Madingley and Coton to those of
Ditton and Cherryhinton, and in another from the
Castle to Barton, Grantchester and Trumpington.
The outward portion of the Fields was almost exclusively arable and tilled in small plots by individual
owners.

Between the arable land and the houses were the
common pastures, consisting of low-lying marsh. Next
the river grass-land reached from the brook at Sturbridge
to St Clement's parish. Then a strip of pasture, now
occupied by College grounds and the Town Greens,
stretched along the river from Northampton Street
to the Mills, and was known as Long Green. Above
the Mills were Sheeps Green and Coe Fen. Lastly
the commons known as Coe Fen Leys and Swinecroft
extended from the river to the Hills Road and
northwards almost as far as Downing Street.

William Harrison, writing about the year 1577, says
'Cambridge hath not such store of medow ground as
may suffice for the ordinarie expenses of the towne and
universitie, wherefor the inhabitants are inforced to

provide their haie from other villages about.' As arable land without pasture is of little use a high value was attached to the right of pasturage in the commons. Exactly what these rights were was a debatable matter. In early times, no doubt, they were customary and attached to the ownership of houses in the borough. In 1583 by a bye-law of the Corporation they were limited to such persons as were resident within the liberties in a tenement 'which of oulde time hath bene used for a dwellinge house': if the house or tenement had been divided among several tenants only the occupant of 'the chiefe mansion howse' was to have common on the Greens. In an ordinance of 1624 the privileged commoners are described as occupiers of ancient tenements 'having of old time broad gates,' which looks like an interpretation of the obsolete word 'hagable.'

Hired labour, which since 1349 had generally taken the place of the enforced services of the old system, was expensive. Sheep-farming required few hands, and wool had become the principal export of England. Throughout England, and expecially in East Anglia, which had become a centre of woollen manufacture, farming was revolutionised, and there was a strong tendency to convert arable into sheepwalks and to 'enclose' what had once been common land.

After 1500 there are constant complaints of the over-stocking of the Greens at Cambridge and attempts on the part of the Corporation to 'stint' the number of sheep, cattle, horses and swine which any individual might put on them. From an ordinance made in 1583, it appears that Aldermen were allowed greater privileges in the use of the commons than other householders. Probably this was an usurpation of the Town bureaucracy, symptomatic of more and worse to come. The poor, ousted from the commons and deprived of employment in tillage, justly suspected the dealings of the bailiffs. The religious houses had once alleviated their distresses by wages or charity: now their lands

had fallen to well-to-do corporations or individuals.
In 1549 it was complained that one townsman had
enclosed and built upon some land, formerly belonging
to the Barnwell Canons, which used to be open field at
Lammas. In another case a piece of common land at
the end of Jesus Lane had been enclosed, whereby the
Corporation was enriched but the 'hole inhabytaunts
of the towne' injured. There was a strong feeling
among the poorer classes that the commons should be
let and the profits applied to their relief. In a rude
ballad of the time addressed to 'the false flattering
Freemen of Cambridge, open and secrete enemies of
the poore,' Jack of the Style says:

> I coulde have been content
> Ye shold have put to rent
> (So they had been well spent
>   In susteyning the pore)
> Your osiers and your holts,
> Your pastures for your colts,
> But now, lyke foolish dolts,
>   Ye shall have them no more.

The outbreak at Cambridge was simultaneous with
the rising in Norfolk, which was headed by Robert
Ket, the Wymondham tanner. These disturbances
were not rooted in general political or social grievances,
but in the local distress caused by enclosures, and the
Government was more than half disposed to sympathise
with the peasants' cause; but the Norfolk rising was
too serious to be leniently regarded. The suppression
of it was committed to John Dudley, at that time Earl
of Warwick. He was son of Edward Dudley, Empson's
partner as financial minister of Henry VII, and earned
for himself the popular hatred which his father so well
deserved; as Duke of Northumberland he has already
been introduced to us on the occasion of his disastrous
visit to Cambridge at the accession of Queen Mary.
He was at Cambridge in August and in the same month
relieved Norwich and dispersed the rebels. The Town
accounts for 1549 tell us of considerable charges for

watchmen in 'the commocyon tyme,' and for a scout who was sent to Thetford; the University also hired armed men and armour. Some of the Norfolk rebels who were brought to Cambridge and lodged in the Tolbooth prison managed to break out; but the Treasurers' item 'for carrying out of Gallows and for a new Rope' seems to imply that others were less fortunate.

At Cambridge, on July 10, a hundred persons or more met together with a drum and proceeded to pull down the fences of an enclosure at Barnwell belonging to one of the bailiffs. The Mayor and the Vice-Chancellor were on this occasion allied in preventing further mischief, and with difficulty pacified the rioters. Both Town and University, assisted by Cecil, afterwards Lord Burleigh, shared in obtaining a general pardon for the local offenders, and the Duke of Somerset, at that time Protector, wrote a temperate letter to the Mayor and Vice-Chancellor recommending gentle dealing in order that 'the difference may be tryed betwixt the ignorant and the learned, the rude and the taught.' A Commission was appointed to redress the grievances, and a long list of 'Complayntes at the Insurrection' was drawn up, which gives particular evidence of the extent of the encroachments.

The disturbances of 1549 were the occasion of some rude pasquinades expressing the feelings of the oppressed poor. One of them, cast in the form of Skeltonian distichs, is a dialogue between the supposed leader of the hedge-breakers, Jake of the Style out of the North, and his sturdy, simple-witted followers. Jake opens the talk by protesting his innocence of the charge laid to him of having slain a man.

> Wher as thy make me a murderer
> And of death a furderer,
> I take God to witnes
> I am of it giltles,
> For as I am a true speaker,
> I am but a Hedge-breaker.

By night he takes company with him and casts 'hedge and dyche in the lake,' *i.e.* the river. He submits the justice of his case to his fellows. Robbyn Clowte answers:

> Methought it but a playe
> To see the stakes fast straye
> Down into the Raye,[1]
> Swymming evermore awaye,
> Sayling towarde the càstyll,
> Lyke as they would wrastyll
> For superyoryte
> Or els for the meyraltie.

Tom of Trumpington is of the same mind:

> Sothe, syr, down to Chesterton
> Great store of stakes be gone
> Swymmyng thither one by one,
> Glad they have escapyd,
> And not of the bayles attached:
> Wherfor they hied them hense
> Paying yet no toll pence.

Buntynge on the Hill points to the offenders:

> Syr, I think that this wyrke
> Is as gud as to byld a kyrke.
> For Cambridges bayles trulye
> Gyve yll example to the cowntrye,
> Ther commones lykewyses for to engrose
> And from poor men it to enclose.

Peter Potter dwells on the hardships of his class:

> The poor saye god blesse your harte,
> For if it contynewyd they shuld smarte.
> The wyves of it also be glad,
> Which for ther cattell lyttel mete had.
> Some have but one sealy cowe,
> Wher is no hay, no straw in mowe.
> Therfor it is good conscyence, I wene,
> To make that comon that ever hath bene.

Sim Slater sees better times coming in the downfall of the bailiffs:

> Now shall I keep styll my cowe.
> For Ioye singe I Hey nonynow.
> The bayles thynke for to have all.
> I truste ons they will have a fall.

[1] *Raye*, old pronunciation of Ree, one of the names of the Cam.

Viro admodum Reverendo
HUMPHREDO BABINGTON
SStæ T.P. Collegii Trinitatis Socio
Seniori Dignissimo Ejusdemq,
Benefactori, & Fautori meritissimo
Viro spectatæ Fidei, & Probitatis
eximiæ Hanc Tabellam humili
limè, offert Consecratq, ex de
bitâ observantiâ
David Loggan.

The Prosp

The Prosp

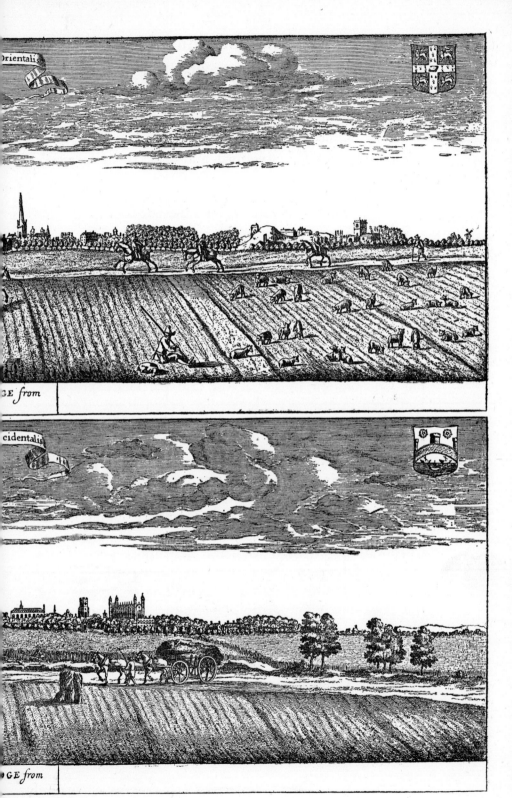

Orientalis

GE *from*

cidentalis

GE *from*

gan's "*Cantabrigia Illustrata*")

Jake ends the debate by counselling his fellows to go home before daylight:

> Lesse the bayleves do you spye,
> Or els sergeants with burbolts bryghte
> Chaunce at youe to have a flyghte.

He is bound for Stamford and bids them farewell. His last words are:

> Common to the commons again I restore,
> Wherever it hath been yet common before.

Jake and his moonlight friends happily had their will, and Cambridge, blest with open spaces which give it health and recreation, may gratefully acknowledge its debt to them for restoring 'common to the commons.' But this battle was renewed many times, and down to the days of the Municipal Corporations Act (1835) there were 'baylies' who 'pinched'[1] pieces of common: one of the complaints against the old Corporation in 1833 was that corporate property had been improperly alienated to corporators. On the walls of St Andrew's churchyard, Barnwell, we may still read of the valiancy of Mr Jacob Butler, in 1752, in resisting the encroachments of the Corporation, every member of which took oath on admission not to abuse the commons or permit them to be abused. Often the benefit of the poor, honestly enough, was alleged as ground for the enclosure. In 1579 the Corporation proposed to make a temporary enclosure of Jesus Green in order that the profits arising from letting it should go towards providing a hospital for the poor and giving employment to the idle; but the University objected and nothing was done. Again, in 1627, it was ordered that the same Green, with the same object, should be let for seven years, and in 1631 the Privy Council sanctioned the letting of it for ten years. In the plague year, 1666, the Corporation petitioned Parliament to be allowed to take in forty

---

[1] To 'pynche' the commons is the expression of Harry Clowte in the ballad above quoted.

acres of Coldham's Common and there to erect pest-houses. As late as 1841 the reformed Town Council made a serious proposal that the larger part of the commons should be enclosed and let as building ground or for market gardens. Fortunately the general indignation which found expression at a meeting in the Guildhall put an end to the scheme.

Enclosures, no doubt, had a good deal to do with the distresses of the poor in the sixteenth century, but other causes were at work to produce unemployment, and no adequate remedy was provided until the close of Elizabeth's reign. The eye of the State was fixed rather on the ' sturdy beggar,' who was a danger, than on the ' impotent poor,' who were merely an incumbrance. The first occasion on which we hear of anything like organised relief at Cambridge was in 1556, a year marked by plague, death and high prices resulting from the depreciation of ' testons,' the base coins issued by Henry VIII. The authorities of Town and University made an assessment for the relief of the poor : collectors were appointed, and the church-wardens of the several parishes made returns of the sums to be paid by each parishioner and of the number of poor to be maintained. This was a purely local provision to meet an exceptional difficulty, and probably there was no legal method of enforcing payment of the cess. An Act of Parliament of 1563 made poor rates compulsory, and another in 1572 directed that dwellings should be provided for the impotent and aged poor. In 1576 it was enacted that materials were to be provided ' for setting the poor on work ' : the stock was to be delivered to them to be worked up in their homes. In 1578 there was talk of using the site of the Grey Friars' house for building a hospital for the poor. In 1581 the Mayor and Aldermen were empowered to build a house behind St Clement's Hostel (on the south side of St Clement's churchyard) ' to set pore men on works and in reformacion for Idle persons according to the statut.' But the first real attempt to carry out the provisions of the Act was made in 1596, when a 'house of correction'[1] was made at the joint charges of the Town and University, and stock was purchased for giving employment to the poor. In 1628 this house was in St Andrew's parish outside Barnwell Gate. In that year Thomas Hobson, the famous Cambridge carrier, conveyed certain messuages in the same parish to trustees for the purpose of building a house or houses on the premises, ' as well for setting poor people to work as for a house of correction for rogues, beggars and other poor persons who should refuse to work.' This workhouse, generally known as the Spinning House, existed until 1901, when it was taken down, and the site has since been occupied by the Borough Police Station. Until the year 1808 wool and flax were still kept there for the employment of the inmates, and the master was a woolcomber. After 1722 workhouses were provided in the several parishes and labour was made a test for relief: the vagabond class were separated from the genuinely destitute and sent to the house of correction. The parish workhouses were usually cottages, and some parishes kept several of them. By order of the Poor Law Commissioners in 1836 the parishes were united for the purposes of poor relief, and in 1838 the Central Union Poorhouse in Mill Road was built for 250 inmates. Several of the parish workhouses, now applied to other uses, still exist.[2]

[1] The name 'house of correction' seems unfortunate, for the purposes were mainly charitable. The accounts of 1597–8 show that in that year the 'apparrell' of 'the children,' which included 'shirts, sheets and hose,' as well as 'bedding,' cost about £25. The lease of the house cost £25, building and repairs about £41, implements and stock about £38, and the wages of a 'fustian weaver' £26. Other items brought up the total to £192.

[2] On the subject of Cambridge Workhouses and Poor Law Administration see the valuable paper of Dr Stokes in C.A.S. *Communications* xi. 70–142.

Chapter XIII.

The Days of Elizabeth

In Cooper's *Annals of Cambridge* the pages allotted to the reign of Elizabeth are more than those given to all preceding times down to the death of Henry VIII, and the spaciousness of the time might well warrant a corresponding space of print. At a time when Religion took new forms, when, for the first time in its history, warfare in defence of English liberty touched the heart of the people, when population multiplied, and when with the growth of commerce wealth was accumulated and the standard of comfort was vastly raised, when new ideals, social and political, were preparing the way for the revolution of the following century—when these things were making England anew, it will be asked what part did Cambridge Town play in the national drama. And the annalist's answer will be singularly disappointing. About the thoughts and doings of Cambridge townsmen in these stirring matters he will tell us almost precisely nothing. The University is rent with division about Pope and Protestant, State Church and Independency. Cambridge churchwardens, obedient to order, deface images or destroy rood-screens; but there is nothing to tell us of the heart-searchings which may or may not have found expression in pulpits or in private circles. In 1588 there was 'post-haste and romage' all over England in anticipation of Spanish invasion : the Town treasurers charge in their accounts for 'corseletts, gorgetts and gunnes' certain sums which are trifling compared with the expenditure on presents to Lord North, and there, for them and for us, ends the record of Cambridge's contribution to the national defence. It by no means follows that Cambridge was undisturbed by such happenings. Simply, evidence is lacking.

The old war with the University throughout the reign was waged with increasing acrimony, and perhaps had a larger part in the townsmen's thoughts than issues religious or political. So far the Parliamentary representatives of the borough had been local tradesmen who had been quite ineffectual in obtaining redress of their constituents' grievances. Now the Town enlisted a powerful champion. For the first time since the sheriff had been removed from his control of the borough we begin to understand that there is a shire of Cambridge which has some interest and concern in the town which is its centre. With the Tudor dynasty there came into existence a new social class—the county magnates, who drew their wealth from the profession of the law or from civil employment under the Crown. In Cambridgeshire, hitherto destitute of a local baronage, parks are enclosed and country seats arise. The new office of Lord Lieutenant, created in the reign of Mary, superseded the duty of the sheriff in raising the shire levies, and to the new military authority were open opportunities of interference in burghal matters which the sheriff lacked.

In the year 1568 an unprecedented order was made by the Corporation giving the status of aldermen of the borough to Roger, Lord North and five other gentlemen of property in the county. Lord North had been elected knight of the shire in 1555, and was re-elected in 1558 and 1563. His father, Edward, first baron North, an eminent lawyer in the time of Henry VIII, was representative of the county in 1541, and Lord Lieutenant in the first years of Elizabeth's reign; he purchased a large estate at Kirtling, near Newmarket and built a stately mansion there, of which only the gate-tower remains. Roger succeeded him in the title in 1564. He was a man of character and intelligence, distinguished as a soldier and diplomatist, an intimate friend of the Earl of Leicester, and held in high regard by the Queen, whom he entertained with great magnificence at Kirtling in 1578. In 1569 he was appointed Lord Lieutenant of the county, and in 1572 was chosen High Steward of the borough. As Lord Lieutenant he was from the first a strenuous defender of the liberties of the Town in its contentions with the University. There is a letter of his, addressed to the Vice-Chancellor, and dated Dec. 5, 1569, in which he refers to the conduct of some student who had used 'evyll and fowle wordes' to the Mayor. He adjudges 'the varlet' to stand in the pillory for three hours with one ear nailed to the same, and to ask the forgiveness of the Mayor on his knees; but afterwards, to pleasure the University, he remitted the ear-nailing. In the Armada year he gave much offence to the Vice-Chancellor and Heads by charging the scholars with musters. In that year he was dwelling in Cambridge at the Falcon Inn in Petty Cury. The Town was profuse in its gratitude. Yearly presents were sent to him. Silver-gilt cups followed one another in an unceasing stream: at one time 'an oxe,' at others 'wethers' were bought and driven to Kirtling: kettles, pails, feather-beds, frying pans and an astonishing quantity of household ware were purchased at Sturbridge for his use.

The liberality of the townsmen to their wealthy neighbour was handsomely repaid by Lord North. The first occasion for his services was in connection with an order, made by the University in 1574 and allowed by the Privy Council in the following year, prohibiting 'showes of unlawfull, hurtfull, pernicious and unhonest games' within a circuit of five miles from the town. In 1580 a certain Robinson obtained from Lord North and the county magistrates license for games, which may have been stage plays, at a place called Howes

on the Huntingdon Road; but on the representation
of the University the license was withdrawn. The
battleground was then shifted to Chesterton, 'which
towne,' as the Vice-Chancellor and Heads complained,
'hath and doth continually annoy our University,'
as, indeed, it did until the middle of the nineteenth
century by its maintenance of billiard-rooms unlicensed by the Vice-Chancellor. In this vexatious
town a football match took place between 'certain
Schollars of Cambridge and divers of Chesterton,'
whereat the Chesterton party, having laid 'divers
staves secretly in the church porch,' picked quarrels
against the scholars and broke their heads, insomuch
that 'divers of them were driven to runne through the
river.' The head constable of Chesterton, Thomas
Parish by name, so far from keeping the Queen's
peace, called on his fellow townsmen to beat the scholars
down: for which miscarriage he was put to ward by
the Justices in the Castle gaol. In the next year the
Vice-Chancellor and Heads made a decree forbidding
scholars to play football, except in their several colleges,
with strangers or scholars of other colleges.

The dishonest game of promiscuous football being
thus reduced within limits of respectability, a worse
trouble befel the University rulers in the matter of
bear-baiting, and the scene was again Chesterton.
On Sunday, April 22, 1581, the Vice-Chancellor
sent one of the proctors with a bedel and others of the
University to inhibit a bear-baiting there, and they
found that the bear had been baited in sermon-time
between one and two o'clock in the afternoon. The
Vice-Chancellor may be acquitted of any Sabbatarian
scruples in the matter. Sunday being the day usually
consecrated to bear-baiting, none but precisians were
likely to set up the Decalogue against it. But when
the bear-ward was commanded by the University
emissaries 'to cease from that disordered pastime'
he replied that he had warrant from the Justices, and

encouraged by Richard Parish, brother of the constable, and a certain 'Long John,' he declined to commit himself to the bedel's custody, and in the *mêlée* which ensued the unfortunate bedel ' was violently thrust and shoved upon the Beare, in such sort that he cold hardly keepe himself from hurt.' To the remonstrances of the proctor the head constable insolently replied that he knew a Justice, not far off, before whose door he might and would bait the bears, the Vice-Chancellor himself looking on and doing what he could.

Though in the result the Parish brothers were committed to the Gatehouse at Westminster and were compelled to submit themselves to the University authority, Richard, who seems to have been a notorious ' bruiser,' gave more serious trouble in 1591. On September 15, being in the ferry-boat between Chesterton and Sturbridge Fair, he attacked and wounded certain scholars, and being arrested by a Master of Arts was rescued by the prentices in the Fair. The bedel who was directed by the Vice-Chancellor to secure Parish declined the job, ' as well in respect of his own weakness as of Parishes outrageous violences,' and it was committed to two more muscular members of the University, a B.A. of Trinity and a singing man of King's. Parish was in attendance on Lord North and the Justices at the Sessions held in the Castle when he was arrested in Bridge Street as the Justices were coming from the Castle; but the followers of Lord North and the magistrates drew their weapons and rescued him. The scholars raised the cry of clubs, and an affray took place in which Lord North was somewhat roughly used, and the same night the inn where he sat with the Justices at supper was beset by a mob of scholars with clubs and drawn swords. Parish, who escaped in the confusion, was found behind a house near the Round Church, and was seized by a number of scholars and carried to the Vice-Chancellor's lodging. Lord North complained to the Privy Council,

H

charging the scholars with having concerted their attack on him and designing to murder him. What was the upshot of the matter we do not know.

From football, bear-baiting and blood-letting it is but a step to play-acting, and that last step in its provocations was taken by the townsmen of Chesterton in 1592. Certain 'light persons,' of whom one Dutton was the principal, advertised a performance there by setting up 'bills' on college gates, and affirmed that they had license from Lord North. The Vice-Chancellor thereupon gave strict charge to the constable of Chesterton to withstand the proposed exhibition and to warn the inhabitants not to give the players entertainment. Unfortunately the order was 'slendarlie executed, or rather wholly neglected,' and the 'Enterludes' were played in a private house. Lord North's reply to the representations of the Vice-Chancellor on the matter was that the powers given to the University to inhibit such performances were 'no perpetuitie': and there the matter seems to have rested. The victory apparently was not on the academic side, for in the same year we find the Town making payment to the players of the Queen and of Lord Strange.[1]

James I, whose addiction to play-acting, cock-fighting and baitings of bulls and bears was notorious, was of a mind that the recreations of royal geese were not to be squared with the pleasures of ganders vicinal to the University. In 1604 he issued an order confirming that of the Privy Council in 1575 and, among 'unprofitable and idle games,' specifying bull-baiting, bear-baiting, common plays, public shows, interludes, comedies and tragedies in the English tongue, as well as 'loggets and nine-holes.' Chesterton therefore might still be indulged with plays in the learned

---

[1] Dutton was the name of two brothers who acted in the company of the Queen's players. Shakespeare belonged to Lord Strange's company, and in 1592 the second part of 'Henry VI' (the Contention) was acted by them. 'Loves Labours Lost' was probably written in 1591.

THOMAS HOBSON THE CARRIER

languages while His Majesty was entertained with the
English comedy of *Albumazar* in the Hall of Trinity,
in 1615. Indeed plays in the colleges, sometimes in
their chapels, were not only tolerated but encouraged
as an element in University education, and at one
college (Queens') performance in them was statutably
obligatory. To 'common plays' and professional
actors the University turned a face of stone. In 1600
one Pepper, B.A. of Corpus, for performing in an
interlude at the Black Bear, 'with an improper habit,
having deformed long locks of unseemly sight and
great breeches undecent for a graduate of orderly
carriage' was condemned by the University to have his
hair 'powled,' and was suspended from his degree.
Even the players of the Queen of Bohemia, King
James' daughter, were refused permission to perform
in the University in 1630.

The interference of the University in the long-
accustomed diversions of the townfolk was perhaps
more resented than any other badge of their servitude.
In defiance of the edict a bull-ring, on Pease Hill, was
made by the Town in 1604, was 'set up' again in
1633, and 'set downe' in 1662. Cock-fighting persisted as a prohibited but popular sport, immemorially
associated with Shrove Tuesday, until the end of the
eighteenth century. It took place on the Market Hill,
and in 1727 the Vice-Chancellor forbade students to
attend there. In 1759 two of the town constables—
one of them bearing the redoubted name of Paris—
were convicted of neglect in preventing it.

Between 1501 and 1597 the Town treasurers on
fifty-seven occasions account for payments to players,
who acted under license from the King, the Lord
Admiral, the Lord Chamberlain, or various noblemen.
For entertainments by 'minstrels,' or 'waits,' constant
payments were made from the first years of Henry VI
to the last of Charles II. In early times the per-
formers were strangers to the town—minstrels of the

King or Queen, the Duke of Bedford or of Gloucester, &c.; sometimes they are described as the waits of Lynn or Bury. The King's 'jogguler' gives performances in 1533 and 1536, and tumblers visit the town in the days of Elizabeth. Such 'shows' were given by command of the Mayor, and usually took place in private houses. It is likely enough that the 'minstrels'' performances were rudely dramatic; but the first mention of 'players' is in 1501, when the Queen's company came to Cambridge. Stage plays were commonly acted in inn-yards—at the Saracen's Head, the Falcon or the Black Bear. Before the royal order of 1605 the University (like that of Oxford) used to resort to the inept 'Danegelt' expedient of subsidising the players to stop away: e.g., in 1583 the Vice-Chancellor gives the Queen's company fifty shillings, 'forbidding them to playe in the towne and so to ridd them cleane away.'

It was long before the Wise Men who ruled the University arrived at the conclusion that eternal spring is not ensured by building walls round cuckoos, and that discipline is not best served by dulness. They learnt the lesson at Sturbridge Fair. In 1701, the Mayor having licensed the performance of a company of actors at the Fair without the Vice-Chancellor's sanction, sixty-two Masters of Arts were enrolled to assist the proctors in preventing a breach of the University privileges. The booth which served as a theatre was demolished, and Doggett, the actor, was sent to gaol. In the 'music speech,' delivered by Laurence Eusden in 1714, he complains that at Midsummer Fair

'We puppet shows receive and banish plays.'

Defoe, writing about 1723, mentions puppet shows, drolls and rope-dancers, 'though not considerable,' among the diversions of Sturbridge Fair. A petition from the Town and County that plays might be acted in the Fair was rejected by the House of Commons in

1737. In 1748 we hear of Hussey's Great Theatrical Booth at the upper end of Garlic Row, but the exhibition seems only to have consisted of singing, dancing and fireworks. In 1772 there was a regular theatre at the end of Cheese Row, at which plays were performed. Soon afterwards the so-called Sturbridge Theatre, which was situated on or near the site of the old Barnwell Theatre, was built and licensed by the Vice-Chancellor. It was open for three weeks during Fair time and belonged to a Norwich company. The performances were of a high class, and on bespoke nights were attended by the Lord Lieutenant and the Members for the Town and University. Dr Farmer, the well-known Master of Emmanuel, and his ' Shakespeare Gang,' regularly occupied the part of the pit which was known as the Critics' Row. There was a fatal fire at the theatre in 1802, in consequence of which it was pulled down, and the Barnwell Theatre was erected in its place in 1806. This was only open in vacations, and its old glories had long departed from it when, in the last quarter of the nineteenth century, it was converted into a Mission Hall. By an Act of 1844 it was ordained that no theatre should be licensed within fourteen miles of the town of Cambridge—so including Newmarket and Royston—except with the consent of the Chancellor or Vice-Chancellor, and in 1856, it was enacted that no performances in theatres in the borough should take place without the consent of the Vice-Chancellor and Mayor. On the infrequent occasions when a travelling company visited Cambridge, it acted at the Guildhall. In 1894 the University renounced its right to license theatres and plays, and in 1895 the present Theatre, under the joint direction of townsmen and members of the University, was opened in St Andrew's Street.

Any account of Elizabethan Cambridge would be defective if it omitted to say something of the optical presentations of the town by Richard Lyne in 1574, and John Hamond in 1592. No town in England, with the possible exceptions of London and Oxford,[1] can boast a plan which offers so vivid a conception of its appearance in the later decades of the sixteenth century. Both these plans are pictorial, representing the town as seen from the south, and have much the effect of a view taken from an aeroplane. Lyne's view, which measures about 17 by 12 inches, is to a large extent imaginative. He shows swine feeding on Swinecroft (otherwise St Thomas' Leys), horses on Newnham crofts, cows and sheep on meadows near the Wilderness of St John's, and corn growing high on what is now Christ's pieces. He shows the wooden and plank bridges crossing the river at the Backs and at the end of Silver Street. Near Fisher's Lane there is a boat in mid-stream dragging a net, and in the meadow westward of King's there is a gentleman in trunk-hose angling in the river. In Magdalene Street he marks the grating in the road where once a bridge called Cambrigge crossed a branch of the Cam. He shows a pump in the lane at the east end of Great St Mary's church, later known as Pump Lane, and the Market Cross with its domical covering, which had been removed before the time when Hamond's plan was made. But Lyne's is no accurate plan. It has no regard for scale: the most important buildings are drawn without any attempt to show their actual appearance. The Castle is shown as a stately structure with a large central tower and two smaller ones.

Hamond's plan[2] is a very large one, measuring 3 feet 11 inches by 2 feet 10 inches, and is contained in nine sheets. It is drawn as accurately to scale as a pictorial plan can be, and as a rule it faithfully reproduces the appearance of buildings as Hamond saw them. So minute, indeed, is his accuracy, that in the case of colleges and more important buildings he distinguishes

[1] The bird's-eye plan of Oxford by Ralph Agas is dated 1578, and his view of London was made about the same year as Hamond's of Cambridge.

[2] The central sheet of Hamond's plan is shown on a reduced scale on the first end paper of this book.

slated roofs from leaden and ashlared walls from walls of plaster or clunch. He sees and marks sundials, flower beds, dovehouses, tennis courts, the shambles in the Market, a stile at a churchyard entrance, a crane on the river bank, a pump-handle projecting from a wall. Unlike Lyne he is completely realistic: he notes things just as they were in 1592.[1] The Castle mound is there; but instead of Lyne's fantastic fortress we see only mouldered walls and an isolated gatehouse. The Great Court of Trinity is a chaos of old, irregular work not yet reduced to the ordered plan set forth by Nevile. Most interesting are the survivals from past time. Emmanuel, since 1584, has occupied a corner of the wide site of the Black Friars, which is all but empty in the plan of 1572; but the grounds which Sidney Sussex occupied after 1596 are bare of habitation, except some insignificant buildings which may well be relics of the Grey Friars. Especially noticeable are the old inns, not named in the plan, but easily recognisable by their long court yards. A good many of them stood on sites once occupied by University hostels, and, no doubt, retained the hostel buildings. These boarding houses for students were once very numerous, some of them large and possessed of courts, halls and offices on the scale of colleges. Dr Caius enumerates twenty which existed within his recollection, and all of them had ceased to have an independent existence when he wrote in 1573. Among the inns, recognisable in the plan, which occupied hostel sites and apparently incorporated hostel buildings were:

> the New Inn, or New Angel Inn, on the site of St Mary's Hostel, now of the Senate House;
>
> the Dolphin, in Trumpington Street, at the N.W. corner of the entrance court of Corpus,

---

[1] In one instance Hamond anticipates history. He shows the tower of Great St Mary's church completed as it is seen to-day; in fact, it was not finished until 1608. His picture was made from a builder's plan, and the churchwardens' accounts of 1591 show that reproductions of such a drawing were then being circulated on collecting cards.

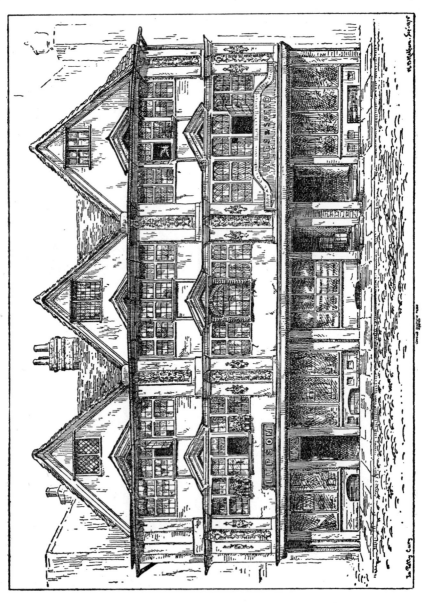

OLD HOUSES IN PETTY CURY IN 1876

formerly St Bernard's Hostel: this was distinct
from the Dolphin mentioned below;

the Rose and Crown Inn, also called Wolf's
Tavern, in the Market Place, occupying the
position of St Paul's Hostel: this was one of
the largest and most famous of Cambridge
inns in the seventeenth and eighteenth centuries;

the still existing Castle Inn, opposite Emmanuel,
formerly Rudd's Hostel: this Hostel was
given to Peterhouse in 1283 by its founder,
Hugh Balsham, Bishop of Ely.

Other well-known inns of Hamond's time and recognisable in his plan were:

the Black Bear in Cordwainer Street (Market
Street), the yard of which remains as Market
Passage;

the Dolphin at the Bridge Street end of All Saints'
Passage, where Cranmer once lived with his
wife, daughter of the hostess;

the Bull, or Black Bull, still existing;

the White Horse, next the Bull: this was the meeting
place of the early Reformers, 'the Heretics.'

This Cambridge of 1592, for all its college splendour
and municipal dignity, is still strangely rustic in appearance, a city of barns and byres. Besides the large
vacancies left by the eviction of the Friars there are
wide spaces of green in the middle of the town. In
the neighbourhood of Green Street (which did not
then exist) there is open field between Trinity Street
and Sidney Street, and there is another bare expanse
between the Ditch and St Andrew's church. On the
westward side of the river, except where it is interrupted
by a paddock belonging to King's, the Town green
occupies all the bank from Queens' to St John's. There
is farm land or void ground from the corner near
Merton Hall to the neighbourhood of Mount Pleasant,

and the Castle is bordered on its northern and eastern sides by corn-rigs, where a man with a team of horses and oxen is shown guiding the plough.   Times were perhaps not wholly changed since the occupant of the Castle, Sheriff Picot, required the loan of burgess ploughs nine times in the year.[1]

[1] On the subject of Lyne and Hamond consult the text (J. W. Clark and A. Gray) and facsimile reproductions in *Old Plans of Cambridge* (1921); for hostels see Dr Stokes' *Medieval Hostels* (C.A.S. 8vo Publ. xxix.; and for Cambridge inns, *Cambridge Described and Illustrated* (Atkinson and Clark), 71–76.

THE TURK'S HEAD COFFEE HOUSE
(now Matthews' Café).

CHAPTER XIV.

James I and Charles I

JAMES I made three state visits to Cambridge during his reign, and the Town was a humble competitor with the University in the adulation and gifts bestowed on the monarch, whom it described as ' that pierles and most noble Prince and morninge starre.' On royal visits, which are multiplied in Stuart and Hanoverian times, so much ink has been expended by contemporary annalists that more may be spared here. So far as relates to Cambridge Town the reign of James may be summed up with the formal obituary that he slept with his fathers and that his acts are recorded in other Chronicles than these.

But one event in his reign calls for mention. On September 30, 1615, died Stephen Perse, M.D., a Fellow of Caius College. Like the founder of his College, he was a Norwich man, and he had practised medicine at Cambridge, with so much success that by his will he left legacies amounting in the total to above £9000. In the town he possessed the grounds of the Austin Friars, a lease of the White Canons' lands, and houses in several parishes. He was a liberal benefactor of his College, in the chapel of which he was buried and is commemorated by a large monument. With the College the Free School which he founded was intimately associated: the Master and four Senior Fellows were appointed supervisors of his will, and to them successively was committed the governance of the School.

Hitherto the only schools, other than private ventures, had been those maintained for choristers at King's, Trinity and Jesus Colleges, the last of which was abolished by Queen Elizabeth's Commissioners. Other Cambridge boys, besides the choristers, were taught in the school at King's. Two members of the University, shortly before the date of Perse's foundation, had bequeathed each a sum of 100 marks towards establishing a grammar school in the town, and Dr Perse willed that his executors should use their endeavours to obtain these sums for the use of his School. The School House was to be built within three years after the Founder's death, and was to contain dwellings for the Master and Usher. Instruction was to be free. The scholars were to be one hundred and no more, and they must be natives of Cambridge, Barnwell, Chesterton or Trumpington. Dr Perse endowed six fellowships and six scholarships at Caius College, and directed that in election to them preference should be given to such as had been instructed for three years at least in the school. Near the school he directed that 'several low tenements of one room apiece' should be built for the habitation of six alms-folk.

Under its first masters the Perse School flourished greatly. Among its earliest scholars was the good Jeremy Taylor, Bishop of Down and author of *Holy Living* and *Holy Dying*. After 1687 a decline began. For more than a century the Caius trustees regularly appointed some of the Fellows of the College to be Master and Usher, and as their interest was in University matters and many of them held country livings, their duties to the School were neglected. To the Perse Fellowships and Scholarships any but Perse boys were elected. In 1731 there were but ten boys in the School. In 1787 the School was shut up, but re-opened in the following year as the result of an agitation started in the *Cambridge Chronicle*. Though the income of the Trust had greatly increased in the latter part of the eighteenth century the Master and Usher still received stipends of only £40 and £20 respectively, as directed in Dr Perse's will, and until 1804 the surplus was appropriated by the College. The houses of the Master and Usher were let to outsiders, and in 1806 the Trustees handed over the School House to the University to house the Fitzwilliam collection. In 1836 an information in Chancery was filed against the Trustees, and a revised scheme for the distribution of the funds and management of the School was sanctioned by the Court. The School premises were rebuilt in 1844. The Master and four Senior Fellows of the College continued to be trustees until 1873, when by an Order in Council a Board of Governors was constituted, partly chosen by the College, the University and the Borough Council, partly co-opted. At the same time a Girls' School was established out of the Trust Funds. The School was removed to its present site in 1891.

Between February and November, 1630, the town suffered from a grievous visitation of the plague. In that year, of 617 deaths from all causes, 347 were of the plague. The University was dissolved, and the colleges were deserted. Dr Butts, Vice-Chancellor and Master of Corpus, writes, ' Myself am alone, a destitute and forsaken man, not a Scholler with me in College, not a Scholler seen by me without.' To make matters worse there was threatening of famine. The inhabitants of the neighbouring villages would neither suffer anyone to leave the town nor come themselves with provisions. Dr Butts says of the town, ' There are five thousand poor, and not above an hundred who can assist in relieving them.' To receive the infected forty booths were put up on Midsummer Green, where they were attended, day and night, by a German physician. ' Besides constables we have certain ambulating officers who walk the streets, day and night, to keep our people from needless conversing, and to bring notice of all disorders.' Horsemen were also hired to range the adjoining fields in harvest time, and to keep ' the disorderly poor ' from doing mischief. A collection for the relief of the poor brought in £164.

Various schemes for the drainage of the Fens were

mooted in the reign of James I, but were met with strong local opposition, especially from the Town and University, as likely to interfere with the navigation of the river between Cambridge and Lynn, and no progress was made with the projects.[1] In 1631 they were revived by the Earl of Bedford and a company of promoters, called the Adventurers, and a contract was made at Lynn, providing that the navigation of the rivers should not be impeded, and that the University, as well as the towns of Cambridge and Lynn, should be represented on the Commission of Sewers. The work was begun but interrupted by the Civil War. It was resumed in 1649 and carried out in the reign of Charles II.

In 1653 Oliver Cromwell was himself an Adventurer, and sent a troop of soldiers to repress the violence of the Fenmen when they assembled to throw down the dikes near Swaffham and Bottisham. In 1633 he was M.P. for the borough of Huntingdon, and won popularity by his opposition to the Earl of Bedford's scheme. It is likely that it was his action in this matter that recommended him to the people of Cambridge. They chose him as their representative in Parliament on March 25, 1640, and re-elected him on October 27 to the Long Parliament, which assembled later in the

---

[1] There is an excellent ballad (early seventeenth century) on this matter, given at length in the *Cambridge Portfolio*, too long to print here more than the first two verses. It is entitled 'The Powtes (*i.e.* eel's) Complaynte uppon Drayninge of the Ffennes in Cambridgeshire.'

Come, brothers of the water,
    And lett us all assemble
To treat upon this matter
    Which makes us quake and tremble.
For wee shall rue, if it be true
    That ffennes be undertaken,
And where there grewe both sedge and redes,
    They'll now feed beeffe and bacon.

They'll sowe both pease and oates
    Where noe man never thought it,
Where men did rowe with boates,
    Ere undertakers bought it.
But, Ceres, thou looke towards nowe
    Lett wylde oates bee their venter;
And lett the frogges and mierey bogges
    Destroye where they doe enter.

same year. The order passed in 1452 and renewed in
1601 required that no one should be chosen burgess
in Parliament unless he were resident in the town,
and there is a tradition that at this time Cromwell lived
in the White Bull yard in Bridge Street. Probably
it was with a view to his election that he got himself
admitted as a freeman on January 7, 1640. He was
nominated by the Mayor, who had the right of appoint-
ing one freeman. Something of the same kind had
happened in 1621, when Sir John Hobart was elected
burgess in Parliament and on the same day was made a
freeman.

In 1625 the old plan of choosing a burgess by a
delegated number of the townsmen was abandoned,
and the election was by 'the greatest part of the
burgesses.' Under Stuart kings the evil practice had
grown up of accepting for the representation of the
Town persons 'recommended' by the Court or by
powerful noblemen. In 1557, when the Duke of
Norfolk, High Steward of the Town, made such a
recommendation, the Mayor and Corporation withstood
the request, and the electors made an independent
choice. In 1614 they chose Sir Robert Hitcham, on
the nomination of Lord Chancellor Ellesmere, High
Steward of the Town, and dispensed with the condition
that he should be a resident. In 1625 when Lord
Keeper Coventry made a similar request for his private
secretary, a Mr Thompson, the Corporation again
yielded, but gave him a qualification by admitting him
as a freeman. At the first election of 1640 Cromwell
was returned in company with a nominee of Lord
Keeper Finch. At the later election the Lord Keeper
nominated two persons, but neither of them was
returned. The choice of the electors fell upon Cromwell
and John Lowry, one of the Four and Twenty, and
afterwards an alderman. As Lowry became a colonel
in the Parliamentary army and in 1648 was appointed
a member of the High Court of Justice to try the

King, the election was meant to be a rupture of the royal leading-strings. Momentous issues depended on the choice of each elector if the fact be, as tradition reports, that Cromwell's return was decided by a single vote.

The fame of Cromwell's preachings at Ely, it seems, had preceded his coming to Cambridge, and had won for him the favour of the Puritans there. Since 1600 Puritanism had become a power in the Town—especially in the aldermanic body. At Trinity church, which had come to be regarded as the church of the Town, as St Mary's was of the University, an afternoon lecture-ship had been established and was supported by the voluntary contributions of the townsmen. It was the practice for the Mayor to entertain the minister at dinner on lecture days, and in 1657 the Town made him an allowance towards the expense. The lecturers, who were chosen by the contributing townsmen, invariably belonged to the Puritan wing of the Church. The popularity of their discourses gave serious uneasiness to the Bishop of Ely and the University authorities. In 1624 the townsmen desired the election of Dr Preston, Master of the Puritan house of Emmanuel. Against him the Heads of Colleges proposed a candidate who was supported by the Bishop. King James offered Dr Preston a bishopric if he would consent to withdraw from the competition; but in vain. Preston was elected and ' preached all his time and did much good.' Before this, in 1619, the King had issued an order that ' no new-created lectures or sermons ' should be preached in any church in the town which should draw away scholars on Sundays from Divine Service, or on weekdays from attendance at lectures. The 'Town Sermon,' as the Trinity lecture came to be called, was held at the same time on Sundays as the University sermon at St Mary's, and was not preceded or followed by the usual service of the day. On that ground it was suppressed, with the natural result that the lecture was given in another church, St Botolph's. In 1629 the King, as a compromise, allowed the continuance of the Trinity lecture, with the condition that it should be followed by the Prayer Book service and catechising.

On January 10, 1642, after his futile attempt to arrest the Five Members, the King left London, never to return to it until the eve of his trial and execution. In March he was at Newmarket, and from thence travelled to Nottingham with a company of nobility, taking Cambridge on his way. Though the visit was unexpected he was welcomed with much ceremony by the University powers. Far different was his reception in the town. A single item of money laid out on the King's footmen is all the record in the town accounts of an occasion which in former years had been attended with so much cost and ceremony, and in the same year's accounts expenditure on 'proclamacions for establishing true Religion' and 'concerning the Troops' and 'sending out scowts' are evidence that the Town was actively committed to the Parliamentary cause. As the King passed through the streets 'women and others in the towne followed his coach, humbly and earnestly intreating that he would return to his parliament, or they should be undone.'

In the first stages of the Civil War Cambridge was the base of the armed forces of the Eastern Counties Association, which was formed in December, 1642. The town was of the first military importance, as commanding the roads which connected East Anglia, a stronghold of the Parliament, with the Midland Counties, where the royal army was operating in 1642, near Edgehill and Cropredy Bridge. A large gun, called a 'drake,' was placed on the Bridge. The Castle, commanding the river passage, was strengthened by adding to the height of its ramparts and throwing up bastions on its eastern side. Stone and timber, provided for the rebuilding of Clare College, were seized and employed for the purpose. Garret Hostel Bridge and five college bridges were destroyed, and a breastwork was put up at the end of Jesus Lane. On August 17, 1642, five days before the King's standard was raised at Nottingham, the Houses instructed Cromwell, the Mayor and Aldermen to raise train-bands and volunteers and to suppress risings. In February, 1643, on intelligence of the approach of a royal army, Cromwell, at the time Captain of Horse, raised a force of 30,000 men for the defence of the town. When the alarm was removed they were dismissed, but a garrison of one thousand remained. The hastily raised troops were an undisciplined mob. One troop refused to advance when commanded ; whereupon Lord Grey of Wark caused them to be surrounded, made them dismount, threatened to shoot them, and after disarming them, discharged them. In March, 1643, Lord Essex issued orders to the troops that they should not offer any damage to the University buildings in which they were quartered, but there is abundant evidence that the orders were little respected. Furniture was burnt, monuments in chapels were defaced, and the scholars' property was stolen and offered for sale in the Market. The University preacher on his way to St Mary's was mobbed by soldiers.

The University, or most of it, was royalist to the core. Before the King's standard was raised it was sending its plate and money to him, and arms were being brought into the colleges. Of fifteen chests full of arms the Mayor seized ten, but the rest were smuggled into Trinity. Some townsmen who had obtained muskets made a practice of firing into the windows of the scholars. In the streets scholars were liable to be assaulted or stoned. No scholar was allowed to pass out of the town unless he had a voucher from a townsman that he was 'a confider.' When Cromwell took Burleigh House and despatched 200 cavalier prisoners to Cambridge the Cambridge Committee were

HOLY TRINITY CHURCH IN 1815

embarrassed by the numbers, and found a danger to the town in ' the Correspondence and Intelligence they held by resort of Scholars to their Windows and Chambers.' The *Querela Cantabrigiensis*, a royalist and querulous account of Roundhead misdoings at Cambridge, says that ' when the King's Prisoners taken at Hilden house were brought famished and naked in triumph by Cambridge to London, some of our Scholars were knockt down in the streets, only for offering them a cup of small Beer to sustain Nature, and the drink thrown in the kennel, rather than the famished and parched throats of the wicked, as they esteem'd them, should usurp one drop of the creature.'

With the battle of Naseby, June 14, 1645, the threat to Cambridge practically ended. Yet in the following August the King was at Huntingdon, and his soldiers looted the town and neighbourhood, and even advanced towards Cambridge. But the town was filled with the forces of the Association, and the King retired to Oxford. When he surrendered himself to the army at Holmby House in Northamptonshire Charles was conveyed thence by Cornet Joyce to Newmarket. On the way he stopped for three days at Childerley, where a painted and panelled room in the manor house is shown as that which he occupied. As there was a likelihood of a demonstration in his favour if he passed through Cambridge he was taken through Trumpington on his way to Newmarket.

There was a last flicker of royalism at Cambridge in 1648, at about the same time as the abortive rising in Kent and at Colchester. It was brought about ' by some disgracefull expressions in the Schools against the Parliament and army, which their friends not enduring pull down the Orator and Moderator; thereupon they fall to blowes, the Royall Townsmen assisting the schollars of their party.' The scholars of Trinity ' did gallantly,' but ' the Parliamentiers prevailed ' and a few were killed.

CHAPTER XV.

From the Commonwealth to the Revolution

So far as concerned the Town of Cambridge the Commonwealth period passed in profound quiescence. Even the ancient feud with the scholars died down. Cambridge accepted the victory of the Parliament, perhaps with satisfaction, more likely with an indifference which was converted into annoyance when the burghers found themselves burdened with the maintenance of the army encamped on Triplow Heath. If the civic authorities 'put out' the King's arms in the Town Hall in 1650 they showed an equal readiness to paint them in again in 1661, and the bonfire for the victory of Worcester, which was lighted by the Mayor's orders in the Market Place in 1651, was not a more sincere mark of rejoicing than the four bonfires which in the same place heralded the Restoration.

The Mayor and Corporation, almost all of them 'Parliamentary,' remained undisturbed in their offices. One of their first cares was the provision of 'preaching ministers.' A commission of the townsmen reported a lamentable state of affairs. The provision for the maintenance of the clergy was in all cases miserably inadequate. Most parishes had no parsonages; ten of the fourteen had no parsons. To remedy these deficiencies the commissioners recommended that six of the churches should be disused and that the parishes to which they belonged should be united with others. St Andrew's church was said to be ready to fall for want of repairs.

The blast of Independency had effectually scattered 'scandalous and insufficient ministers,' Anglican and Presbyterian, but failed to breathe spiritual life into

dead bones. Erastianism, which might be thought
to have perished on Laud's scaffold, raised itself in a
more intolerant form under the control of Parliament,
and against any form of religion which was unlicensed
by the State it waged truceless war. Quakers were
turned out of the town as vagabonds. When George
Fox passed through Cambridge, in 1655, he was
assaulted by a mob of scholars—apprentices, as he calls
them, in the trade of preaching—and nearly dragged
from his horse, and when he walked through the streets
there was 'a bustle' from which he was rescued by a
friendly Mayor. For their misusage the Quakers
themselves were mainly responsible. They harangued
in the streets against Universities, learning, tithes,
and the clergy. One of them, William Sympson,
went about naked and barefoot, sometimes putting on
sackcloth and besmearing his face, and denounced the
dominant religion; but the Mayor 'did nobly' in
putting his gown upon him and taking him into his
house.

In 1655 we hear for the first time of a stage-coach,
which went between Cambridge and London thrice a
week each way. It housed at the Rose Inn, Cambridge,
and the Swan in Gray's Inn Lane. The fare for
passengers was ten shillings, and letters and parcels
were carried. Before this time travellers to Cambridge
from the North and from Norfolk commonly went
by river from Lynn, and, until the end of the eighteenth
century, the network of rivers and channels in the
Fens provided transport for heavy goods. The business
of horse-hiring was a lucrative one in Hobson's day,
when most students travelled by road. More important was his trade as carrier 'betwixt Cambridge
and the Bull' in Bishopsgate Street: his cart was drawn
by a team of eight horses.[1] There were two routes to

---

[1] J. Taylor in his *A Way to find out all Carriers* (1637) says: 'The Waggons or
Coaches from Cambridge do come every Thursday and Friday to the *Black Bull*
in Bishopsgate Street.' Another Cambridge carrier, who came every Thursday,
lodged at the Bell in Coleman Street.

London—by Bishop's Stortford and by Ware—and
both were bad roads, as Pepys often comments.   Pepys,
usually travelling on horseback, once by coach, generally
covered the distance in two days; if he accomplished it
in one he started at four in the morning and arrived at
eight or nine at night.

Letter posts throughout the country were established
by the Government in 1635; but, perhaps at an earlier
date, the University sent its letters to London by
licensed carriers, and its privilege was retained in successive Acts of Parliament.   About the year 1749
the University had eleven licensed carriers, five of them
plying to London.   Parcels weighing less than an ounce
were charged twopence.   The Post Office mails were
uncertain.   In 1648 there was no direct service to
Cambridge.   Letters were left at Royston and for-
warded thence, sometimes after delay, and sometimes
a London letter reached Cambridge by way of Scotland.
It was considered a surer plan to send them by carrier.
A daily post to London was established in 1741, but
in 1763 no post went out from Cambridge on Saturdays
or came in on Mondays.   In 1785 the Cambridge
bags were sent to and brought from Bourn Bridge.
Though in 1741 two stage-coaches and three stage-
waggons went weekly to London, there was no delivery
of letters by mail-coach directly between Cambridge
and London until 1792.   The Wisbech coach which
began to run in that year performed the journey
between London and Cambridge in seven hours and
a quarter.

When the Convention Parliament of 1660 was
elected with a great majority in favour of the restoration
of monarchy, the county of Cambridge went with the
tide and returned two members who ' declared for the
Parliament and a King and the settlement with the
Church,' and ' carried it against all expectation.'   Not
so the borough of Cambridge, which promptly chose
for its representatives the two candidates who had been

defeated in the county. On May 11, 1660, King
Charles was proclaimed in customary manner by the
Mayor, John Ewin, but, as Samuel Newton remarks,
' more audibly ' by the Town Clerk. Amid ' accla-
mations of Joy from all sorts ' the Mayor, Aldermen
and Bailiffs, in retrospect and in prospect had small
ground for jubilation. Hardly one of them could be
called a royalist, and most of them were rigid Puritans.
In face of the popular feeling they could scarcely do
less than restore the King's arms on the conduit in the
Market-place, but with the proviso that the Corporation ought not to bear the charges and that no precedent
was thereby created. As the attitude of officialdom in
many boroughs was much the same as at Cambridge
the royalist Parliament of 1661 passed an Act for the
regulation of corporations and appointed commissioners
of enquiry.

The Cambridge commissioners held their first meeting
on July 19, 1662, at the Black Bear inn, the yard of
which forms what is now Market Passage. The Mayor
and Aldermen were first summoned, and were required
to swear allegiance and supremacy and to take the oath
that the Solemn League and Covenant was unlawfully
imposed. The Mayor and five Aldermen took all the
oaths without demur : two refused the oath against
the League and Covenant : the other seven declined
to appear : John Lowry sent word that he was weary,
as he well might be. Next, the twenty-four Common
Councilmen were summoned : eleven took all the oaths,
nine refused them, and the rest absented themselves.
The two bailiffs refused to appear. The absentees
and those who declined to take all the oaths were
ejected from office. So too was the Mayor, Thomas
French, who had shown inordinate activity in exercising
Parliamentary train bands and in displacing royalist
clergy, and was suspected by his own party of dubious
dealings with public funds ; moreover he attended the
lecture at Trinity church and ' came little at St Mary's.'

He died the next year. In his room Samuel Spalding was appointed: he had already been Mayor in 1630 and again in 1655, and though he had been a sequestrator of royalist estates and had served on the committee for ejecting 'scandalous ministers,' his honourable character marked him to the commissioners as 'faithful found among the faithless.' The Corporation Act which authorised the intrusion of the Government in municipal affairs was passed against the wishes of the King; but it gave an ill precedent for the similar invasions of 1685 and 1687.[1]

In the summer of 1665 and again in 1666 the town was visited, for the last time, by plague. Sturbridge Fair was interdicted by Orders in Council, and forty acres of Coldham Common were enclosed for the purpose of putting up pesthouses. The population of the town was probably less than 6000. In 1665 the deaths in all the parishes and from all causes were 413, and in 1666, excluding the parish of St Giles, they were 797. Though, next to London, the Eastern Counties and Cambridge in particular are said to have been the worst centres of the disease, it is likely that the visitation was less severe than in some earlier plague years. Defoe's imaginative pictures of the Great Plague in London have left such a nightmare impression of its horrors that we are surprised to find so little to correspond with them in contemporary Cambridge records. Alderman Newton, whose diary has so much to tell of the small occurrences of Cambridge life, has little more to say than that 'severall dyed heere in Cambridge and at the pesthouses of the sicknes.'[2]

But the orders issued by the magistrates in 1665

---

[1] See the valuable article by Dr W. M. Palmer, 'The Reformation of the Corporation of Cambridge, in 1662,' C.A.S. *Communications* xvii. 75–132.

[2] An indication of the intensity of the pestilence in one quarter of the town is supplied by the register of burials in the parish of St Michael. Between June 11 and September 7, 1666, there were buried twenty persons, of whom all, save one, died of the plague. In each of the two following years only two burials are recorded. Between August 7 and August 10 there died Thomas Manisty the elder, his wife and daughter; between September 2 and September 6 were buried the wife of Thomas Manisty the younger and three of their children.

give a lively picture of conditions in the town in plague time. 'The pesthouse' and 'the keeper's house' were to be aired and cleaned, a 'searcher' was appointed for those who died, and watchmen were to carry provisions and other necessaries for 'the phesecian' and others. The searcher was 'an ancient woman that had the infection': the order implies that she was still infected, or infectious; isolation of individual cases seems not to have been attempted. The Mayor and the High Constable were directed to visit the pesthouse 'at a distance, once a week, taking the windward side, to know their wants.' A horse and an old cart carried the infected persons and household goods to the pesthouse at two o'clock at night, and the infected at the pesthouse loaded and unloaded the cart and drew it and buried the dead. Watch and ward was set at all passages, especially towards London, and some ends of the town were 'cast up and boarded.' Most of the inhabitants were watchmen in their course, two or three attending at every passage, 'and one at least of them to have good discression,' and all to be armed. Huts were built of boards for the watchmen, and the orders of the magistrates were made in writing and fixed upon the posts. Coaches and waggons from London were interdicted and letter-carriers were forbidden and stopped: the postboy was ordered to fume his letters, and another man delivered them. Harvest men were not admitted without testimony. Families which were suspected to be infected and refused to remove to the pesthouse maintained themselves, but those at the pesthouse were maintained at the public charge: evidently whole households, sound as well as sick, were deported. 'Visited' persons at the pesthouse after 28 days stay there since any of their family had died were allowed to return to their houses in the night, 'and made fires to air them, and smoked them with unslaked lime, keeping their doors and windows shut for a while, and after two hours set them open to let out the smoke.' The watchmen were not allowed to watch two nights together for fear of sleeping. Nobody was allowed to come into the town after ten o'clock at night.[1]

The pestilence was most violent in Bridge Street and from thence to Sidney College. Of twenty-two deaths registered in the fortnight, November 2–16, 1665, fifteen were of plague and ten of the fifteen in the parishes of St Clement and St Sepulchre. In the spring of 1666 there was a breathing-space, when for some weeks no plague deaths occurred: but in the summer of that year there was a fresh outbreak with much increased violence. There were no deaths in the Colleges for the reason that the whole place was ' disuniversitied,' the scholars having been sent to their homes. It is recorded of Thomas Tenison, afterwards Archbishop of Canterbury, that he continued to reside and attend his cure at St Andrew's church. Such heroism in the parish clergy was so marked that, in gratitude, the inhabitants presented him with a handsome piece of plate.

The reign of the restored King, at least until its last years, passed as an after-dinner's sleep. Visits of royalties and magnificos, with such gratulatory addresses as occasion demanded of the civic authorities, make up a large part of Cooper's *Annals of Cambridge* in those years. That they were years of trading prosperity there is no ground to doubt; and there is as little room to doubt that, while individuals waxed in wealth, those seeds of corruption were planted in the corporate body which were to grow to rankness in the century and a half which followed. Now begins the fatal practice of making honorary and non-resident freemen. Twenty-two county gentlemen were elected in 1679; the freedom was granted without payment to sixty-five non-residents and eighty-five inhabitants

---

[1] The magistrates' orders are from the note-books of Sir Thomas Sclater, J.P. for Cambridgeshire, 1660–1684. They are printed in Dr Palmer's already mentioned article, C.A.S. *Communications* xvii. 121–2.

of the town in 1688. In 1788 seventy-three non-residents were made free by payment of one guinea each. The object in all cases was to swamp the independent electorate of the town. The nominees of 1688 were all in the interest of the Romanist, Henry Jermyn, Lord Dover, who in that year was forced upon the Town as its High Steward. Yet there was some cockle of the rebellious feeling of 1642, which had to be weeded out of the Common Council when Cambridge, like other towns, was called upon to surrender its charter to the King in 1684. Two aldermen and seven councillors were displaced. On November 11, 1684, the Corporation surrendered to the King's Most Sacred Majesty all the franchises conferred on it by previous charters, and with all submission implored him to re-grant them with such restrictions as he thought fitting. The new charter, which was granted on January 3, 1685, gave the Crown power to remove any of the town officers at pleasure. The cost of obtaining it was £258, with £1 additional to the Waits 'for playing when the charter was read.' As in the case of the musicians in *Romeo and Juliet*, their instruments were soon turned to 'melancholy bells': for a month later Charles died in the height of his triumph.

The same bells rang and trumpets sounded on February 9, when James II was proclaimed at the Cross in the Market Place; and, five days later, in their loyal address, the Townsmen protested that all their lives and fortunes were his Majesty's, and that they would be daily employed to preserve him in his royal seat. Which loyal attitude of mind was by them duly maintained until they saw reason for changing it. Trouble for the Town began on September 16, 1687, when Alderman Newton received a visit from Alderman Blackley, who desired him to go with him to call on the Mayor, Isaac Wallington, for the purpose of presenting a letter signed with the King's seal manual and requiring the Corporation to choose the same Blackley as Mayor for the coming year. Blackley was a reputed Papist, and once had been a Quaker. A certain Mr Fage had already been chosen for the mayoralty, and refused to resign his claim. The Mayor and three aldermen were despatched to the Court to represent how matters stood, and, for the time, the King was satisfied and ordered that the election of Mr Fage should be proceeded with. But much worse was to come. On April 8, 1688, came Orders in Council for removing the Mayor, five Aldermen, twelve councillors, and the Town Clerk, and substituting in their places nominees of the King. Nathaniel Crabb was appointed Mayor in place of Fage. In the same month six more aldermen and twelve more councillors were removed, and successors were appointed in their stead. All the new officials were dispensed from taking the usual oaths.

On May 8 the new Corporation obsequiously voted an address of thanks to the King for the Heroic greatness of his royal mind shown in his Declaration of Indulgence, and certain 'mean and inconsiderable' dissenters of the town had no better sense than to present a similar address acknowledging the King's 'moderation and tenderness.' On June 11, three days after the Bishops were committed to the Tower, there were bonfires and bell-ringings for the birth of the babe who was to be known in history as the Old Pretender, and on October 8, a month before William's landing at Torbay, the Mayor and bailiffs presented to the King an address testifying their 'utmost aversion to exchange a just and most indulgent Monarch for a slavish submission to any foreign invader.' What talk of warming-pans went on outside the Council Hall, what prayers were breathed in private for the restoration of Reformed Religion and Law Cambridge annals record not. We may take it that Alderman Newton when he prayed God to make the infant Prince of Wales a blessing to the nation was not the only townsman who coupled with the prayer a thanksgiving for the deliverance of the Bishops. Royal treason had done its worst on August 16, when Blackley was chosen Mayor elect. But he never succeeded to the office. Alarmed by the imminence of William's invasion, James made haste to restore the forfeited charters of the boroughs. On October 22 the Mayor, Nicholas Eagle, summoned a meeting of the Common Council, at which was read the royal proclamation restoring the old Corporation, and Mr Fage was elected Mayor for the coming year. In his term of office he did serviceable work in arresting soldiers of the Scots regiment who were disaffected to the new King.

Following William's landing there were wild scenes at Cambridge, described in Samuel Newton's diary. On December 13 he writes: 'This night, and severall nights before, there were upp in armes a great many in this Towne, some nights 200 or 300, many scholars among them, of the rabble called the Mobile, who at first under a pretence to seek for papists and such who had favoured them and to ransack their houses for armes, at last came to be very insulting and wherever they pleased to enter men's houses and doe them much mischeife.' Next night 'betweene 8 and 9 of the clock at night it was reported by one Turkinton that came from or about Huntington that 5000 or 6000 of the Irish lately disbanded had burnt Bedford and cutt all their throats there, and they were comeing on for Cambridge, to doe the like there, whereupon all this whole Towne was in an uproare and fearfull crying out all about the Towne and all presently upp in armes crying out in the streets Arme, arme for the Lord's sake, and it being a rayny and darke night candles alight were sett upp in all windowes next the streetes, and it was said that they were comeing in at the Castle end, others said they were come in and were cutting of throates, soe that the scare for the present was very great and dismall, many running and rideing out of

Towne to escape the danger, till it was considered how improbable such a thing should bee soe of a sudden, and besides wee were informed from some who came that afternoone from Bedford and that way, and they neither see any Irish nor heard of any such comeing into those parts or this way, and soe the Towne about 10 of the clock that Evening or before began to be free from any such feares.'

On February 18, 1689, William and Mary were proclaimed King and Queen at the Market Cross and elsewhere in the town with the full ceremony which had attended the accession of James.   Trumpets, kettledrums and waits raised echoes of the fanfares of 1685, and 'all the afternoon and at night ringing of bells and at night bonfires' proclaimed with as much noise and perhaps more sincerity the whole devotion of Cambridge to the King whose pretensions its spokesmen had so recently abhorred.

Chapter XVI.

Bureaucracy

WHEN the shouting and the tumult that welcomed the deliverance of the nation from Popery, French shoes and warming pans had died away, Cambridge settled down to a century of humdrum. The electorate had faithfully represented the views of the townsmen in 1640 when, in opposition to the royal nominees, they had chosen as representatives of the borough Oliver Cromwell and John Lowry, both of them freemen of the town. By the Instrument of Government (1653) it was provided that there should be only one member for the borough. Cambridge continued to show its attachment to the Parliamentary cause by electing Richard Timbs, an alderman, to the single seat in 1654 and 1656. The story that Timbs in 1640 introduced Cromwell to the town, and procured his admission as a freeman, is perhaps unveracious, but that he was a Cromwellian is not to be doubted. In December, 1658, after the Protector's death, he was once more returned—this time along with the former representative, John Lowry. Poor Lowry fell upon evil days after the Restoration, being charged, on insufficient evidence, with peculation as collector of taxes during the interregnum, and in 1662, declining to take the oath of allegiance, he was turned out of his aldermanship. Excepting John Pepys, M.P. 1694–1696, Timbs and he were the last resident freemen elected to serve Cambridge in Parliament. To the Convention Parliament of 1660 the burgesses returned Sir Dudley North and Sir Thomas Willis.

Both these men had qualified for election by being made complimentary freemen. They were considerable landowners in the county, North at Kirtling, Willis at Fen Ditton, and were not Cambridge residents. From 1660 onwards the representation of the borough was generally held by county magnates, and elections were swayed less by political considerations than by family interests in which the borough had no active concern. For a century and more the battle was between the clans of Chichely of Wimpole, Cotton of Madingley, Jenyns of Bottisham, Bromley of Horseheath, and others, and the chief interest of the independent electors was to see to it that the candidates came with money in their hands. The choice lay with the Mayor, Bailiffs and freemen, who, under the old conditions of residence in the borough, were not likely to exceed a hundred in number: but the manufacture of honorary freemen, referred to in the last chapter, was vivaciously carried on until the lucrative trade was ended by the Reform Bill of 1832.

Of the manner in which this privileged body exercised the franchise a lively picture is drawn in the evidence gathered by a Committee of the House of Commons in the matter of an election in May, 1708. The Mayor, who was the returning officer, declared that never was there a fairer election; but 'Fair is foul, and Foul is fair,' and one of the candidates was unseated for corrupt practices. Though much of the evidence given to the Committee was false, or at least contradicted, enough remains to show that victorious Pot and defeated Kettle were equally and unmistakably black. It was deposed that Mr Shepheard, father of one of the candidates, was proprietor of the Rose Tavern, that there a club was kept consisting of the Aldermen and Twenty-four, and that the son, by treating them with ' as much wine as would have drowned them,' had been accepted by them as candidate for the borough.

The candidates were Mr Cotton, son of Sir John Cotton of Madingley, Mr Shepheard, a London merchant, introduced by the Cottons, and Mr Bendysh of Foxton.

The two former were Tories, Mr Bendysh a Whig, but political considerations were of secondary interest, and the voters, so far as they were not corrupted, were mainly guided by attachment to one or other of the contending families. Shortly before the election the Corporation had voted the freedom to Cotton and Shepheard; and a round dozen of others, half of them Londoners, who were made freemen at the same time, all voted for them. Cotton and Shepheard were declared duly elected. Bendysh petitioned the House of Commons for the seat of Shepheard on the ground that his return was due to corrupt practices and the unprecedented number of freemen created for the purpose of the election. Two years after the contest a Committee of the Commons decided that Shepheard's election was void, but they did not award the seat to Bendysh. Thereupon Shepheard was returned without opposition.

The evidence supplied to the Committee revealed that fraud, bribery and violence were equally employed by both parties in the contest. The Town Clerk informed several voters who had been fined for breaches of law that their fines would be reduced or remitted if they voted for the Corporation candidates. On the same side voters disqualified by being in receipt of alms were admitted to the poll. Opposing voters were made drunk and then locked up in rooms at inns. A townsman entitled to freedom by inheritance could not induce the Town Clerk to put forward his claim until he pretended that he would vote for Shepheard: but he actually gave his vote the other way. It was alleged that one voter was fetched out of gaol, where ' otherwise he might have remained for his life,' by the Recorder, the Mayor and Shepheard: he owed £44 to the Corporation, which was abated to £24, and he was told that he might be easy as to the rest.

In 1715 there was again an election and again a petition. The Mayor, Charles Chambers, returned

Cotton and Sclater as duly elected. The defeated candidates, Shepheard and Jenyns, petitioned the House of Commons, partly on the ground of bribery, but more especially because the Mayor and others, in violation of the ancient constitution of the Town, had made certain persons free. The Mayor was ordered by the Committee of Elections to allow the petitioners to inspect the Town records; but he refused to do so; for which he was taken in custody by the Serjeant of Arms and was only discharged on his submission. Since 1623 it had been the rule to admit freemen only at what was called a Summoned Common Day attended by at least six aldermen. At a meeting held a few months before the election only five aldermen were present. In order to defeat the Mayor's purpose the other seven wilfully absented themselves, and on the appointed day made an excursion together to Bourn Bridge. Nevertheless thirty-six freemen were admitted by those present, of whom eight were admitted gratis, eight by purchase, and the rest by right. When the Mayor was warned that complaint would be made to the House of Commons, he answered that if those he had made were not enough to carry the election he would make sixty or a hundred more and would ' give Mr Shepheard his Belly-full of the House of Commons.'

There was copious evidence of bribery by both sides, but the Commons unseated Sclater and declared Shepheard duly elected.

In connection with this election a characteristic story is told of Dr Bentley, the famous Master of Trinity. On the foundation of that College there were twenty-four beadsmen, usually old servants of the College, who received pensions and clothing, In 1715 the Master proposed to the Seniority to fill up two vacancies with persons recommended to him by a gentleman of the county: one was an alehouse keeper, the other a man who had made himself notorious as the leader of the Tory mob at the late election. 'To the first,

The Petitioning Vintners &c. ——— &c.

THE VICE-CHANCELLOR AND THE VINTNERS (1786)

who was unknown to them, the Fellows made no objection, but on the mention of the other the whole
meeting started with astonishment: they asserted that
he was the most worthless and notorious character in
the whole town, the universal leader in all riots and
disturbances.   Bentley replied that by his appointment
the College was sure to be protected from rioters, and
added that it was for their interest to oblige gentlemen
of the county.   But when he found that neither his
joke nor his arguments availed he declared that he would
elect this man with the single vote of Mr Brabourn,
an unfortunate personage of impaired intellects, who
was his never-failing supporter.'

If we may judge from the trades exercised by Mayors
in the half century after 1660 that of vintner was
by much the most important, or at least the most
influential.   The licensing of wine-merchants in the
town was one of the oldest prerogatives of the University.   It was frequently called in question by the
Town authorities, but was confirmed and maintained
in the Cambridge Award Act of 1856, and was only
renounced by amicable agreement with the Town in
1890.[1]   Other trades were of minor importance.   'The
Trade of the Town,' writes Defoe in 1723, 'very much
depends on the Colleges, and the Tradesmen may
justly be said to get their Bread by the Colleges.'
The shire, of which the town was the trading centre,
was not, as it has been since the draining of the Fens,
a distinctively corn-growing region: its main wealth
consisted in wool.   In 1720 the Corporation addressed
a petition to the House of Commons setting forth the
hardship of the unemployed poor owing to the decay
of woollen manufacture in the town consequent on
'the almost universal wear of East India goods': yet
at Sturbridge Fair in 1723 the mart of woollen goods
was vast and exceeded all others.   'The river,' said
the Town Recorder, in his address to King James in

[1] See footnote, page 191.

1615, 'with navigation to the sea, is the life of trafficke to this Town ': and so it remained until the last quarter of the eighteenth century. Heavy goods—iron, stone, timber, coal, wine, even the bricks and tiles which for new and better houses were displacing the pargetted fronts of earlier days—all were brought by water from Lynn. Hence it was with much concern that Town and University noted that the navigation by barges was in danger of being destroyed by the silting of the channel between Cambridge and Clayhithe, and in 1781 they combined to petition Parliament to bring in a Bill 'for making and erecting Sluices and other Engines on the said river and cleansing and digging the Shallows.' An Act with these objects was passed in 1783.

Since the introduction of Turnpike trusts, first applied in an Act of 1663 relating to the Great North Road, a good deal of attention had been paid to the improvement of land communications. Before that time roads were mended in a makeshift way by local labour provided by parish guardians, and even University 'scholars' were subject to the service, either in person or by substitute. At Cambridge considerable benefactions for the purpose of maintaining highways in the neighbourhood were left by Hare in 1611, Perse in 1615, and Worts in 1709. Acts were passed in 1674 and 1724 for mending the London–Cambridge roads and collecting tolls. There was a tollgate where the pavement began in Trumpington Street. At a later date (1745) in a petition for an Act to improve the roads connecting Cambridge with Godmanchester and with Newmarket it was stated that many hundreds of waggons passed in September by these roads to Sturbridge Fair.

No doubt the intimate importance of the Fair to the prosperity of the Town was an actuating consideration in the promotion of these Bills. In 1723, when Defoe described it as 'not only the greatest in the whole Nation, but in the World,' Sturbridge Fair

was in the zenith of its glory. 'To attend this Fair
and the prodigious conflux of People which come to
it there are sometimes no less than fifty Hackney
Coaches, which come from London and ply night and
morning to carry the People to and from Cambridge,
for there the Gross of the People lodge: nay, which
is still more strange, there are Wherries brought from
London on waggons to plye upon the little river Cam
and to tow People up and down from the Town and
from the Fair as Occasion presents. It is not to be
wondered at if the Town of Cambridge cannot Receive
or Entertain the Numbers of People that come to this
Fair: not Cambridge only but all the Towns round
are full: nay, the very Barns and Stables are turn'd
into Inns and made as fit as they can to Lodge the
meaner Sort of People.' The vast popularity of
Sturbridge as a trade-mart is attributable to the network
of rivers which found their outlet at Lynn: and Lynn
was the depôt of a great coasting trade with Newcastle
and the Humber on the one hand and the Thames
on the other. Not without reason—the price of coal
being enhanced by a third and likely to go higher—
the Town, in 1702, petitioned the Lord High Admiral
for such convoy as would protect coasting vessels from
privateers. The wares exposed at Sturbridge came
from every part of England. In the Duddery were
wholesale dealers in woollen and cotton manufacturers
from the towns of Yorkshire and Lancashire, as well
as serges and kersies, &c., from Devonshire and the
West: in the Cheapside were represented all trades that
can be named from London; a separate part was assigned to hop-merchants from Kent, Surrey and Essex;
unwrought wool came principally from Lincolnshire
and was bought in great quantities by manufacturers
in Norfolk and Suffolk; hardware was brought from
Birmingham and Sheffield, glass and hosiery from
Nottingham and Leicester. In all Defoe's list of
produce and manufactured goods one looks for any

speciality contributed by Cambridge or its neighbourhood, and vainly: Cambridge produced, made and
sold nothing. The profits to Cambridge Town were
from tolls, fines and the letting of standings for booths:
to individuals the gains to be got from the lodging and
entertainment of some thousands of visitors. The
cost of carriage of goods to and from the Fair must
have been prodigious. Defoe notes that business was
already being conducted on a more economical plan,
which in after times was to be the undoing of Sturbridge, as of other Fairs. ' A prodigious Trade is
carry'd on here by Wholesale Men from London and
all Parts of England, who transact their Business
wholly in their Pocket-Books, and meeting their
Chapmen from all Parts make up their Accounts,
chiefly in Bills, and take Orders: These they say
exceed by far the Goods actually brought to the Fair
and deliver'd in Kind.'

The half-century which followed the Revolution is
generally accounted an age sterile of ideals—perhaps
we look for harvest in seedtime. Admittedly in the
world of politics at Cambridge, as elsewhere, it was a
time when decaying Form was perverted to the basest
uses, and mean private advantage betrayed the common
good. Yet it had its beginnings and its ' movements,'
religious and social, little noticed at the time, but
fruitful for after days. The Declaration of Indulgence
(1687) had the undesigned result of giving a recognised
status and free voice to Protestant Dissent and of
dealing a death blow to the asphyxiating creed of
ecclesiastical Uniformity. In 1659 the Quakers held
their meetings in the house of a shoemaker in Jesus
Lane, but next year a mob of scholars and townsmen
battered down its walls and laid it open to the street.
In 1700 a bequest by Ann Docwra gave them possession
of the Jesus Lane site, where their Meeting House
remains to the present day. In 1687 the Presby-
terians acquired a piece of ground on Hog Hill

opposite the present St Columba's Church, and built a chapel there : but in 1696 a part of the congregation seceded to the Congregational body, which since 1688 had met in Green Street. Another party of the same congregation joined the Baptists in 1721, and at first held their services in ' the Stone Yard,' next to Hobson's Spinning House in St Andrew's Street, on which site they have continued to the present day.

In 1719 died John Addenbrooke, once a Fellow of St Catharine's, and a leading physician in the town. By his will he left £4500 to hire, purchase or erect a building fit for ' a small physical hospital ' for sick persons of Cambridge and elsewhere. For an institution on the most modest scale the sum was inadequate, and the trustees whom he appointed allowed it ' to accumulate ' until 1766. In that year an Act of Parliament was obtained to make it a general hospital : a site was purchased and a building put up and furnished for about £4000. As the total capital remaining in the hands of the trustees after forty-seven years of ' accumulation,' produced an income of not more than £48, voluntary subscriptions were invited for its maintenance, and some large sums were gathered from the Town, County and University. The original hospital was contained in a house of ordinary size in two storeys with garrets in the roof. The present structure dates from 1865, and since that time it has been very much enlarged. Addenbrooke's modest endowment preceded that of Radcliffe's Infirmary at Oxford by half a century, and both as a Hospital and a School of Medicine has been productive of far wider and more beneficent results than could have entered into the visions of the donor.

Another scheme which, like Addenbrooke's, has to the present day continued and amplified the intentions of its promoters, belongs to the year 1703. Before that year there was no provision at Cambridge for the education of children of the poorer classes. The

Perse School indeed existed, and, as its Founder had purposed, it originally gave a gratuitous education to boys indifferently drawn from all classes at Cambridge and in the neighbouring villages. But before the close of the seventeenth century, owing to the incompetence of its masters and the grave dereliction of the trustees, it had completely forfeited the confidence of the townspeople, and those who could afford to pay fees usually sent their sons to private schools. It is hardly necessary to say that schooling for their daughters had not so much as entered into their thoughts. In 1698 the Society for Promoting Christian Knowledge was founded, its primary purpose being the establishment of schools for the free education of poor children. One of its five founders was Simon Patrick, then Bishop of Ely. To him is attributable the adoption of the scheme at Cambridge, and foremost among its supporters was William Whiston, the able but erratic Lucasian Professor of Mathematics. As approved by the ministers of the Town churches the design was ' to train up poor children in the Knowledge and Practice of the Christian Religion as profess'd and taught in the Church of England.' The boys were to be taught ' to Read, Write and Cast Accounts,' the girls ' to Read, Write and Work.' All were to be instructed in the Church Catechism and Liturgy and to be brought to church twice every Lord's Day at the beginning of Divine Service. Masters and mistresses were appointed sufficient for the education of 260 children, and fifty children were clothed as well as educated. There were six schools, each with its own master or mistress. The schools were supported by voluntary contributions and an annuity of £30 left by William Worts in 1709. At the beginning of the nineteenth century both the number of the schools and the standard of education had fallen. In 1808 there were indeed eleven schools, but in nine of them, kept by mistresses, the boys were only taught to read and the girls to work: in the two kept by masters the more advanced boys learnt writing and arithmetic. The Charity Schools of 1703 were the lineal progenitors of 'the Old Schools' of Cambridge, which still derive part of their support from voluntary contributions, and maintain their traditionary affiliation to the Established Church.

CHAPTER XVII.

Social Conditions in the Eighteenth Century

FOR some fifty years after George II ascended the throne
the Mayor, Bailiffs and Burgesses of Cambridge did
nothing in particular, nor is it of historical consequence
whether they did it ill or well. That they ate and
drank at this inn or that : that, as occasion demanded,
they presented humble and loyal addresses to this
George or the other : that they made a gallant show
when they rode in their gowns to open Sturbridge
Fair on horses ' richly caparisoned ' and attended by
redcoat ' Henchmen ': these and the like doings are
they not written in the *Annals* of C. H. Cooper?
And that they exercised the trust reposed in them of
electing whom they would to represent themselves,
but not Cambridge, in Parliament—this also is on
record. Candidates, if they were to be successful,
must be ' Corporation candidates.' The Madingley
Cottons were their prime choice from 1688 to 1752.
At a contest in 1737 the voters were 248, of whom 66
had been admitted freemen a month before the election.

These were the days of Walpole, and it may be
allowed to the Town senators that they were not more
corrupt than their time : and corruption was the in-
evitable outcome of the composition of the electorate.
The Mayor, Bailiffs and Burgesses—such was the legal
style of the parliamentary borough—elected one
another. The Burgesses—in other words the freemen
—determined who should be admitted as freemen,
and also made choice of the Burgesses who should
represent them in Parliament. The Test and Corporation Act required that no person should be admitted
to municipal office who had not, within the twelve

months precedent, taken the sacrament in accordance with the rites of the Established Church. By some unexplained process a Presbyterian was chosen Mayor in 1760 : how he reconciled his conscience to qualifying for office, or how the burgesses reconciled theirs to the omission of the qualification appears not : it was enough that he supported the Corporation candidates. In 1787 it was objected to the Mayor-elect that he had not received the sacrament within the prescribed period.

If the Corporation had no hand in promoting the schemes of social welfare mentioned in the last chapter it may be set down to their credit that some of their edicts give a vivid picture of social conditions in mid eighteenth century. In 1736 they lay down a self-denying ordinance respecting Corporation entertainments on the occasion of proclaiming fairs : the total amounts to £26, not including about 3½ dozen of Port and four bottles of Canary. In 1778, with a grieved sense of the enormity of the offence, they impose a penalty of 20s. on persons guilty 'of the mean and scandalous practice of stealing the Corporation wine.' In 1759 two parish constables are convicted of neglecting their duty to apprehend persons guilty of cock-throwing on Shrove Tuesday. In 1737 they direct that a disorderly person, named Mad Tom, as soon as he can be apprehended, shall suffer 'correction of whipping by the hands of the common cryer,' under which he is to continue until he leaves the town : one thinks of another 'Poor Tom,' who, being likewise mad, was 'whipped from tithing to tithing.' In 1749 it stands recorded that the same cryer disciplined 'ladies' with his whip in the Spinning House : again one thinks of King Lear's 'rascal beadle.' In 1745 they pay an alderman £1 6s. for a ducking chair for scolds on the Great Bridge ; which seems to have been worn out in 1766, when the Chief Constable is charged to make a new one. As late as 1785 they note the want of stocks in many parishes of the town, and direct that in each parish stocks shall be erected for setting Drunken and Disorderly Persons therein.

Whips, stocks and ducking stools seemed to the Corporation the appropriate means of punishing wickedness and vice and thereby making industry and virtue more loveable to the six thousand odd subjects ruled by Bumbledom. Quite otherwise it seemed to John Mickleborough, minister of St Andrew's, who in a sermon preached to the Corporation in 1751 urged the necessity of a general workhouse for the poor. Which monition the Corporation so much took to heart that they requested the several parishes to consider the matter: which recommendation being by the parishes considered, or not, nothing was done until 1790. Workhouse and gaol were convertible terms. In the Spinning House the poor found employment and the disorderly were whipped. In the Town gaol debtors were herded with felons, and in the seventeenth century with 'witches.' It was contained in the same small house, next the Tolbooth or Town Hall, which had been the abode of Benjamin the Jew, and in 1224 was given to the Town by Henry III for a gaol. On the ground floor was 'the hole,' which was intended for criminals, and, when John Howard visited the place in 1776, was occupied by one prisoner, 'a miserable object': above were rooms for debtors and criminals, one of them called 'the cage.' The gaoler had no salary, but had a license for supplying beer to his wards; otherwise he drew his income from fees paid by the prisoners on commitment and discharge and for their lodging. No water was accessible to the prisoners, and there was no court for their exercise. In the Spinning House there was one room for men, two for women offenders, and 'a dungeon or dark room for the refractory.' Lately bedsteads for straw or coverlets had been introduced. Seventeen women were confined in a workroom, 19 feet square, which had no fireplace and no sewer: so offensive was it that it occasioned a fever, whereof two or three died in a few days: whereupon the Vice-Chancellor ordered the rest to be discharged.

Not to any eruption of energy on the part of the Corporation was due the erection of a new Great Bridge of stone, designed by Mr Essex, which in 1754 took the place of the old timber structure, an affair which, as the Pontage book shows, was at all times 'like a German clock, still a-repairing, ever out of frame.' Curiously enough, the Bridge, like the Castle, had never belonged to the town. The county sheriff was its custodian and, when it needed mending, he collected a rate from certain lands scattered about the western part of the shire—an arrangement which probably dated from pre-Conquest times. The process of collecting the dues was troublesome, and the duty was evaded as far as it was possible. The new bridge was built by subscription at a cost of £1327, to which the Corporation contributed £50.

The year 1744 is notable for the appearance of the first Cambridge newspaper, *The Cambridge Journal and Flying Post*, which in its early years described itself as printed 'at the New Printing Office in Cambridge by R. Walker and T. James, next the Theatre Coffee House,' the Theatre being the newly-built Senate House: the Printing Office was in fact a house on the west side of Trinity Street, which was used as the porter's lodge of Caius College. The printers seem to have been London men, and Walker published books in London which were advertised in the *Journal*. The paper consisted of four pages with three columns on a page: the page was rather smaller than one of the Literary Supplement of the *Times*. It contained no local news and no original articles. The contents consisted of a summary of general news and 'advices' from foreign Gazettes and from London, Edinburgh and Dublin journals. In early numbers it gave a good deal of space to ' Advices from the North,' bearing on the rising of 1745–6. In politics it was neutral. In an advertisement it stated that it was distributed by seven men at great expense in a dozen different counties, and sent by post to London and York. In 1766 the *Journal* was assigned by the proprietor, Mrs James, ' together with her whole Stock of Printing Materials, Stationary and Public Medecines to Messrs T. Fletcher and F. Hodson on the Market Hill,' who had started the *Cambridge Chronicle* in 1762. From 1767 the united papers appeared as the *Cambridge Chronicle and Journal*.[1]

It was perhaps not quite fortuitous that the office of the *Journal* was next door to a coffee-house : it is at least noteworthy that in 1771 two Fellow Commoners of the University were indicted at the Sessions for assaulting one of the proprietors of the *Chronicle* in a coffee-house : whereon followed the usual squabble between Town and University about ' conusance.' At any rate popular newsvending and the coffee-house were everywhere twin institutions, though in process of time the newspaper won the birthright of its somewhat elder brother. The coffee-house first came to London in 1652, and rapidly spread to all the larger towns. They were generally kept by Levantine tradesmen, and in London bore such names as the Greek's, the Smyrna and the Turk's Head. At Cambridge two well-known houses were the Greek's and the Turk's Head, the latter being the house with the charming plaster front in Trinity Street, still appropriately known as the Oriental Café. Speaking of the time between 1661 and 1677 Roger North says, ' Coffee houses were but young. At that time and long after there was but one, kept by one Kirk.[2] The trade of

---

[1] C.A.S. *Communications* viii. 347–358, on *Early Cambridge Newspapers* (R. Bowes).

[2] At some date between 1651 and 1671 John Marston, 'in Trumpington Street,' issued a half-penny token having on the obverse the device of a hand issuing out of clouds and pouring coffee out of a coffee-pot into a cup, with three other cups at the side placed on a table.

news also was scarce set up: for they had only the Public (*i.e.* the London) Gazette, till Kirk got a written newsletter circulated by one Muddiman.' Later it became the practice to resort to the coffee house to read newspapers, of which, North says, ' swarms are continually supplied from London.' A German who visited Cambridge in 1710 mentions in his diary that he was taken to the Greek's coffee house, and there ' read all the journals,' and was particularly pleased with a weekly publication called the *British Apollo*. In this coffee house, ' particularly in the morning and after 3 o'clock in the afternoon, you meet the chief professors and doctors, who read the papers over a cup of coffee and converse on all subjects.' The Greek had a coffee booth at Sturbridge fair. About 1760 Dockerell's in Trumpington Street was a famous house of this kind : masters of arts used to occupy the upper, bachelors and undergraduates the lower parts of the room. As a place of meeting for news and conversation the coffee house took the place of the barber's shop, and sometimes the trades were combined. In 1763 John Delaport, ' a hair merchant,' kept a coffee house next Emmanuel College, of which, and his peruke factory in St Andrew's Street, an elaborate advertisement appeared in the *Chronicle*. It contained ' a Library of Books,' and it was promised that Instruments would be provided for the musically inclined. In the garden which was attached to it there was, once a week, an entertainment of vocal and instrumental music, and in a pool guests might catch fish ' and have them drest in the best Manner.' Also the French Tongue might be learnt, cheaply and expeditiously and without a bad accent.

The multiplication and wide dissemination of newspapers were made possible by the improved condition of roads and the comparative regularity and cheapness of vehicular travel. In the views of Cambridge streets which figure in Loggan's *Cantabrigia Illustrata* many riders are shown, but comparatively few wheeled vehicles: carts of two wheels are generally drawn by two or three horses, but four-wheeled carriages by as many as eight. In 1702 Francis Burman, travelling to Cambridge by coach and four, started from London at 5 a.m. and arrived at 8 p.m. In 1724 and 1730 Acts of Parliament were obtained for repairing the road between London and Cambridge, with the result that the journey became more expeditious and cheaper than horseback. Of public conveyances there were various kinds. In 1763 the London Post went out every day except Saturday, and came in every day except Monday. It was probably less rapid than the Fly, a machine ironically described in Johnson's Dictionary as ' a stage coach distinguished by this name to impress belief of its extraordinary quickness in travelling.' The Cambridge Fly started from the Rose Inn at 7 a.m. and professed to arrive at the Queen's Head, Gray's Inn Lane, at 5 p.m.; it saved an hour by not stopping anywhere to dine. It carried four passengers and the fare was twelve shillings. The ordinary stage coach, for four or six persons, ran every week day, and the fare was ten shillings. Once a week there were stage coaches to Norwich and Bury, and a chaise to Yarmouth. There were, besides, horse carriers to London, Ipswich and Kettering, cart carriers to Huntingdon, St Ives and Colchester, and waggons to Birmingham and Leicester. In addition boats plied on fixed days to Lynn and Wisbech. The Cambridge newsmen went into all the adjacent counties, and parcels were taken in at the Printing Office.

Though the highways leading to the town were in tolerable condition, every contemporary account describes Cambridge, apart from the University buildings, as in the last degree sordid, and its streets as narrow, dirty, unlighted and unpaved. Edward Ward, visiting the place in the last years of the seventeenth century, says of it: ' The town is so abominably dirty that

Drawn, Etch,ᵈ & Pubᵈ Mᵃʸ 1809, by Dighton, Charᵍ Croſs.

A VIEW of the TELEGRAPH, CAMBRIDGE.

DICK VAUGHAN, THE DRIVER OF THE 'TELEGRAPH' (1809)

Old Street in the middle of a winter's thaw or Bartholomew Fair after a shower of rain could not have more
occasion for a scavenger than the miry streets of this
famous corporation, and most of them so very narrow
that should two wheelbarrows meet in the largest of
their thoroughfares they are enough to make a stop
for half an hour before they can well clear themselves
of one another to make room for passengers.   The
buildings in many parts of the town were so little and
so low that they looked more like huts for pigmies
than houses for men.'   A rather later visitor, Uffenbach,
reports of it: ' The place is not at all large and about
as mean as a village, and were it not for the many fine
colleges it would be one of the sorriest places in the
world.'[1]   Stirred up by the University and some of
the principal inhabitants the Corporation made an
abortive attempt in 1769 to procure an Act for cleansing,
lighting and paving the town, but nothing was done
until 1788.   Before that time gutters were in the middle
of the street: spouts discharged from roofs on the heads
of passers: shops had been extended by throwing out
projecting windows into the streets, making them so
narrow that two carriages could not pass each other.
In the universal darkness bands of undergraduates
were ' scarcely less ferocious than the members of the
Mohock and Sweating Clubs,' and persons carrying
lanterns were insulted and the lanterns taken from
them.   On winter evenings carriages were usually
attended by a servant carrying a torch.   But private
carriages were few—Gunning says that there were but
three—and for evening visits ladies usually went in
sedan chairs, a specimen of which still exists at Trinity.[2]

   As in villages, the majority of the houses were thatched,
and fires were frequent.   The provisions for extinguishing them remained much as they were in the days
of Elizabeth, when it was agreed between the Town

---

[1] Mayor, *Cambridge Under Queen Anne*, 197, 410.
[2] Gunning, *Reminiscences of Cambridge* i. 293–296.

and the University that each parish and college should provide a certain number of ladders, leathern buckets, scoops and hooks. The hooks were attached to long poles, and their use was to pull down roofs, and for the purpose rings were fixed under the eaves. Such rings may still be seen at several houses, some of which in the eighteenth century were of recent and better construction, *e.g.* the Master's Lodge at Peterhouse and the Lion Hotel. The extinguishing implements were kept in parish churches: there is still a firehook in the tower of St Benet's church, and until recently it hung on the outer wall.[1] Long after the period which belongs to this chapter the Bellman, with dog, lantern and halberd, went his nightly rounds, rousing the sleeper with his ' drowsy charm,' as in Herrick's day :

> 'From noise of scare-fires rest ye free,
> From murder, *Benedicite.*'

In 1723 among the civic dignitaries who went in procession to the opening of Sturbridge Fair, was ' the Bellman in state with the stand on Horseback,' and well on into the nineteenth century he yearly solicited a Christmas box from his ' worthy Masters and Mistresses dwelling in Cambridge ' in a printed sheet of doggerel verse.[2]

Old prints present a fairly lively impression of the amenities of Cambridge streets as they were from the days of William III to the latest years of George III. From the date of Loggan's *Cantabrigia Illustrata* (1690) to that of Harraden's *Cantabrigia Depicta* (1811) and Ackerman's *History of Cambridge University* (1815) the appearance of the principal thoroughfares had undergone little change. In Loggan's time there were no sidewalks. Colleges which fronted a main street protected their gateways by a row of posts. Roof pipes, where they existed, were not carried to

---

[1] C.A.S. *Communications* xii. 232–239, *The Rings under the Eaves of Old Houses* (G. E. Wherry).

[2] C.A.S. *Communications* xx. 33–39, *The Cambridge Bellmen* (Dr Stokes).

the ground; by a bend at their lower end they discharged the rain water to some distance into the street.
No college deemed it necessary to put up a fixed lamp
at its main gate or in interior courts : and what colleges
omitted to do, it is safe to say, was not done by private
individuals. Some dim lighting of the streets was
nevertheless attempted in the reign of Elizabeth. In
1575 the Town and University came to an agreement
that ' for the avoiding of such inconveniences as might
happen in the evenings of the winter quarter, being
dark, as also for lights to be had in the streets in the
same evenings, lantherns and candlelight in the same
shall be had and used within the town yearly from the
feast of All Saints (Nov. 1) until the feast of the Puri-
fication of the Virgin Mary (Feb. 2), in such place and
places and at such charge as the Vice-Chancellor and
the Mayor shall appoint, except such nights as the
moon shall shine.' If Cambridge was not in advance
of London it may be assumed that even on moonshine
nights the illumination was only from 6 p.m. to 9 p.m.
Better class householders were required to ' hang out '
lights from walls or windows, and the ' uneffectual
fire ' was ordinarily a rushlight. A watchman was
appointed by the Corporation to ' cry lanthorn and
candlelight ' : in 1617 he was a tinker and was paid
6s. a year for his pains. He perambulated the streets
calling ' Lanthorn and a whole candlelight, hang out
your lights.' This system lasted until 1672. Then,
if the silence of the Town Treasurer be taken as proof,
Cambridge returned to curfew conditions and ancient
night.[1]

And so, apparently, it remained until the passing of
the already mentioned Act of 1788 for the better
paving, cleansing and lighting of the town. In that
year lamps were first lighted and the first street, Petty
Cury, was paved. The previously existing law (1544)

[1] In 1751 the Vice-Chancellor and Heads issued a decree stating that 'great
terror and apprehension was caused by students who walked the streets with
lighted torches or links' and forbidding the practice.

required individual owners to pave so far as their tenements extended, but only to the middle of the street. The improved paving consisted of rounded cobbles, such as still line the kerbs of some of the less important streets. The lamps were mostly fixed against the walls of houses and colleges, and in day time were removed to be refilled. Colleges which fronted a main street, Emmanuel, Christ's, Sidney, Trinity, and St John's, had lamps on the street side of their gates: the rest had none.

Chapter XVIII.

Bribery and Corruption

In October, 1774, there was an election for the Borough, and therewith a painful awakening of the Mayoral junta to the consideration that the Town contained some hundreds of 'inhabitants' who, not being free 'burgesses,' nevertheless exerted their voices, sometimes decorously in petitions and resolutions, other whiles in inarticulate uproar in the Market Place. Also there came to light the yet more lamentable fact that in the select and hitherto harmonious meetings in the Council chamber and at the Rose Inn there had arisen a discordance of opinion in the senatorial body. There is a minority of the Corporation which is bold enough to assert that Whig Codlin is a better friend than Tory Short: Codlin's principles are altogether loftier, and dissentient Aldermen find his wine, and 'the inhabitants' his beer, even better than Short's. Therefore when the Mayor declared that the two 'old members' were duly returned by the constituency, the mob became 'exceedingly furious.' When a load of Tory beer appeared on the Market Hill 'the populace seized it, broke the casks, let the beer into the kennels, and as the members and their friends were returning to the Rose Inn under the protection of the constables and their assistants, pelted them with the staves of the barrels, and burnt the carriage which brought the beer.' Two loads of Whig beer which afterwards appeared were 'received with loud huzzas and soon drank up.' At night the mob broke the windows of the Mayor, of the Rose Inn and others in the town. One much detested Alderman, who was the Corporation's election agent, was so hurt that he died a few weeks after the election.

Partly, perhaps chiefly, the cleavage in the aldermanic body was attributable to the emergence on the
meridian of Cambridge of a new political star, whose
attraction was much more powerful than the influences
of those lesser and local lights which had hitherto
swayed the electorate. Charles Manners, son of the
immensely popular Marquis of Granby, was M.A. of
Trinity College, and represented the University in
the Commons from 1774 until he succeeded to the
Dukedom of Rutland in 1779. The Rutland family
had recently acquired a great estate at Cheveley, once
the property of the Landwade Cottons, and in the house
there kept up a lavish hospitality. In Parliament
Manners, supported by Burke and Fox, played a large
part in protesting against the taxation of the American
colonies, and in endeavouring to restore peace after
the outbreak of the War of Secession. In 1786 Fox
and Sheridan were presented with the freedom of the
Town. In the crisis of the French Revolution the
Rutlands supported the administration of Pitt, and
Cambridge followed their lead. For good and for
ill the Rutland dynasty ruled unchallenged in the
Corporation for half a century.

At a meeting of the burgesses before the election of
1774, Francis Tunwell, one of the aldermen, moved
that a declaration should be submitted to each of the
candidates that they would endeavour to procure
legislation for establishing a more fair and equal representation of the people in Parliament : for ensuring
enlarged toleration for Protestant Dissenters : for restoring to the American colonists the right of taxation
by their own freely elected representatives : and for
repealing the Boston Port Act, the Massachusetts
Government Act, and the Act for the trial in Europe
of persons accused of offences in America. The Tory
candidates, as supporters of the North ministry which
had passed these Acts, naturally declined to subscribe
to this declaration, and, as naturally, the two Whigs

ADDENBROOKE'S HOSPITAL IN 1811

Drawn by R. B. Harraden, Junr

Etched by Elizabeth Byrne

engraved by William Byrne

signed it. In November, 1775, at a meeting of 'the inhabitants,' convened at the Rose Inn under the presidency of the Mayor, William Weales, a petition to the King was carried by a great majority. Protesting their loyalty and affection to the throne the signatories in temperate language expressed their apprehension of the consequences of 'the most ruinous war begun in America.' The petition was signed by the Mayor, one alderman, all the four bailiffs, eleven of the Twenty-four and 144 other inhabitants. A counter address expressing 'detestation of all Rebellion, Treason and Faction' was presented to the King by the two Borough members, and was signed by ten aldermen and 82 inhabitants. In November, 1776, there was a by-election. Again the Tory was returned by a majority of three to one: the riotous scenes of 1774 were repeated, and the defeated candidate petitioned on the ground of bribery and corruption. Once again, in 1780, the two Tories were elected. Then in 1784 there was an unopposed return. The chosen two were Major Adeane, the former Tory member, and John Mortlock. In choosing the latter the constituency reverted to the ancient practice, in abeyance since 1694, of electing as their representative a resident burgess.

Of John Mortlock, the most capable administrator of borough affairs produced by the old system, a good deal must be said. From 1784 to his death in 1816 he was the undisputed dictator of the Town, and he bequeathed the position to his sons. Between 1785 and 1809 he was chosen Mayor thirteen times. His two sons continued his rule until 1816, and together were mayors in thirteen years, and on the very few occasions when an outsider filled the office he was the nominee of the Mortlocks in alliance with the Rutland party.

John Mortlock was the son of a well-to-do Cambridge draper. Inheriting his father's business he added to it that of a banker and by his courteous and accommodating dealing gained much influence both in the Town and the University, and so prospered that he bought a considerable estate at Great and Little Abington. He was made a freeman in 1778, was M.P. from 1784 to 1788, Recorder in 1788, and Receiver General of the Post Office from 1791. By rectitude, wisdom and benevolence, he won the respect even of political opponents. In business and private affairs his hands were clean: in national concerns, whatever his methods, he sincerely intended what he believed to be the public good: but in municipal politics he was the architect of a system of corruption which outlasted his own time and surpassed in scale the worst misdoings of the corporate authorities for a century before him. His justification was that, the world being out of joint, he had to set it right by whatever tools lay to his hand. To a friend who, agreeing with his politics, disapproved of his methods, he remarked, ' Without influence, which you call corruption, men will not be induced to support government, though they generally approve of its measures.'

In 1780 at a meeting of yeomen and freeholders of the county, held at the Shire Hall, a petition was drawn up and addressed to the House of Commons protesting against the system of administration by parliamentary corruption as absolutely unjustifiable on every principle of good sense and sound policy. The occasion introduced Mortlock to the Duke of Rutland, both of them being among the signatories. Though the petition was aimed against corruption in the Commons and not in the electorate, it might seem a curious text on which to base an alliance which brought about a scandalous debasement of the Cambridge constituency. Mortlock's plans for making the Corporation entirely subservient to himself were from the first deliberate. In opposition to the Aldermen's club, which met at the Rose Inn, he started a rival club at the Eagle and

Child in Bene't Street, an inn kept by one of the Common Council. Here there was a monthly supper and, in alternate months, a dinner followed by a supper. The meetings were attended by the Mayor, the magistrates, the Council and some freemen. The guests, all of whom supported the Rutland interest, did not attend by invitation but, as they considered, as a matter of right, and they paid nothing for their entertainment. Dinners and wine were excellent, ' and plenty of both.'

At first the old device of swamping the constituency with non-resident freemen was liberally employed. Seventy-three were created in August, 1788, by payment of one guinea each. It might seem that it was a needless thing to do, for at an election earlier in the year the Rutland candidate got 41 votes and his opponent only seven. As the total number of residents qualified to vote was about 100 it would appear that it was not considered necessary to call up non-residents. Probably Mortlock was aware that among residents there were always some voters convinced or obstinate enough to require a bribe to induce them to vote to order, and the business was troublesome, uncertain and hazardous. It was easier to corrupt the few, and non-residents were kept in reserve, only to be called up if serious opposition was threatened. So well was it understood that the reserves held the election in their hands that there was no contested election for the borough until thirty years after 1788.

The aldermanic body was small, self-elected, and held office for life. No tales were likely to be told outside the Common Hall and the club dining-room. But the price of an alderman's vote was of course higher than that of the freeman who earned the suffrage by service or parentage; even a Rutland might stick at the cost. Better would it be if for their fidelity to the principles of sound government the Corporators should remunerate themselves out of corporate stock. The

Corporation had considerable landed and house property: it was a simple matter to let it on beneficial lease for nominal sums and long terms to one another or to their friends. It held funds, some derived from charitable trusts, which, in the absence of any public audit of accounts and with the assistance of a well-disposed banker, might readily be apportioned mutually among its members. Magistrates, strict in the enforcement of law where petty offenders were concerned, relaxed their vigilance at the Eagle and Child, and were little disposed to question in the case of others the legality of jobs which were so advantageous to themselves.

Transactions such as these were 'notorious' in 1833, and notoriety implies scandal. To the Corporators of 1788 they might appear to be matters of common practice, justifiable to moderately tender consciences. They were doing what half the corporations in England were doing. There was nothing in the law of their being that constrained them to charge themselves with an active supervision of the concerns of the mere 'inhabitants' of the town. In Tudor and Stuart days the Council had taken some thought for such matters as Poor Relief, the regulation of trade and prices, rules for the market and for the common pastures, and showed a faint regard for paving and sanitation. The Council of 1788 found nothing 'so nominated' in the charters which gave it its privileges. 'The object of the club dinners was to support right principles and to preserve harmony and unanimity among the freemen.' Harmony they presumably got: righteousness is a matter of private interpretation.

While in national history the years between 1780 and 1815 were resonant with great events and echoes of resulting change, the same years at Cambridge produced only incidental sparks scattered by the general combustion and dying as they fell. The townsmen, who had been at variance with the borough oligarchs when the latter supported North's administration during the American war, had no quarrel with the Rutland Club when it ranged itself with Pitt in the Revolutionary and Napoleonic crisis. Cambridge witnessed no such scenes of Republican riot as happened in many towns of England and Scotland. On the contrary, after the September massacres of 1792 there was a violent outbreak of feeling against the Revolutionaries and their sympathisers in England. The Dissenters were generally credited with favouring the opinions of the Levellers, if not of being in correspondence with the Jacobins.

'Almost every evening during the latter part of this winter [1792] there were riotous assemblages, and the windows of many of the Dissenters were broken. A very numerous mob collected one evening, who, after breaking several windows, did great injury to the Meeting House [near St Thomas' Leys]. They were headed by two chimney-sweepers, under whose directions they proceeded to the Market Place and attacked several houses, endeavouring to burst open the doors; this was prevented by some Masters of Arts who came to assist the magistrates. By their united exertions the rioters were dispersed, but not until after the Riot Act had been read. . . . Two men were afterwards convicted at the Town Sessions for a riot and attacking the Meeting House, and were sentenced to fourteen days' imprisonment.'[1]

At a large meeting in the Town Hall on December 15, summoned by the Mayor, an Association was formed for preserving Liberty and Property against Republicans and Levellers; and a few days later, the publicans of the town issued a joint declaration that they would immediately give notice to the magistrates, should it come to their knowledge that any persons in talk or by circulation of seditious books or pamphlets were endeavouring to excite riot or inflame the minds of the populace. On the last day of the year Tom Paine was burnt in effigy on the Market Hill.

War was declared by France in February, 1793, and on war followed high taxation, famine prices, scarcity and consequent disturbances in all parts of the country. In 1795 the King's carriage was pelted

[1] Gunning's *Reminiscences* i. 251–2.

by the mob, as he passed through London to open Parliament, amid cries of ' Give us bread : no War : no Famine.' In July a subscription was raised in Cambridge for providing the poor with bread at the reduced price of sixpence the quartern. Nevertheless, on the 17th of that month,

> 'a mob assembled and seized a lighter laden with flour, which was going down the river to Ely and Littleport, and were preparing to divide the flour among them, when the Earl of Hardwicke and several other magistrates, assembled at the County Sessions, immediately went to the spot, in order to preserve the property of Mr. Howard, the owner of the flour, and on the suggestion of some gentlemen present, it was put in a waggon and carried to the Town Hall, where it was deposited. As soon as Mr Mortlock, the deputy Mayor, heard of this proceeding, he sent for the mealman to whom the flour belonged, and paid him for it, assuring the populace that it should be kept in the Town Hall for the use of the inhabitants, and that an ample supply was provided for them. A handbill was also published, signed by the Vice-Chancellor and deputy Mayor, addressed to the poor inhabitants, informing them that they shall have bread at sixpence the quartern loaf. This had some effect, and they dispersed for that night. On the next day, Saturday, they crowded the market at an early hour, declaring that they would not suffer any regrating or forestalling; about 10 o'clock they seized some meat which they supposed had been unlawfully kept back or taken out of the market, which the Mayor caused to be brought forth and publicly sold. The same was done by many other parcels, till at length the mob increased both in their numbers and demands, and insisted on having meat sold at four pence per pound, which many of the butchers complied with under the direction of the magistrate, who promised that the loss should be made up to them. . . . Mr Mortlock continued on horseback with the mob the greater part of the day; and under the idea that they would not be guilty of any very violent excesses, if not provoked, he determined to risk the appeasing them himself, without calling in the constables or swearing in supernumerary ones, lest anyone over zealous should irritate them, and thereby put it out of his power to preserve tolerable order.'[1]

In the War period, 1793–1815, Cambridge town and county well merited the proud distinction conferred on them eight hundred years earlier by the Anglo-Saxon chronicler who, in a disastrous fight with the Danes, records ' then stood fast the Cambridge men.'

[1] Cooper, *Annals of Cambridge* iv. 454–5.

Even when Napoleon's camp was assembled at Boulogne, and invasion was hourly expected, there was no universal compulsory conscription, such as there was in 1916–1918, but each county was required to furnish a fixed quota of men for the militia and to provide their equipment. In 1796 the county was called upon to find 646 men for the militia, the quota of the town being 48; in 1799 the number required of the town and county for militia and volunteers was 901; in 1803, on the renewal of war after the Peace of Amiens, it was raised to 1564.

In 1794, when the French had over-run all Holland and Belgium, and on the continent were everywhere victorious, the county raised a troop of yeomanry consisting of eighty men and increased the militia by a certain number of volunteers. For their equipment a sum of £4235 was raised by voluntary subscription, and considerable sums were subscribed again in 1803. It may be mentioned that for similar purposes subscriptions had been raised in 1745, and during the American war. In 1799 a Patriotic Association of Cambridge Volunteers was formed to raise a corps for service in any part of Great Britain, 'in case of invasion by a foreign enemy, which was daily expected.' The corps met for military exercises in the Market Place on the first Monday in every month. It originally consisted of 450, and was organised in six companies; later two more were added from Chesterton and Bassingbourn. Another local regiment of volunteers was raised in 1804. There was also a University company consisting of 146 officers and men.

As has been mentioned in Chapter XVII, visitors to Cambridge, before and after 1700, were struck with the meanness and village-like appearance of the town. It had scarcely changed its character in 1800. Nothing can be clearer than the pettiness of the town, nothing more surprising than its stagnation during the eighteenth century. In 1801, when the first decennial census was taken, the population (apart from the University) was 9276—slightly more than that of March to-day. There was indeed an increase since 1749, when a house to house enumeration showed a population of 6131; but it is a striking fact that the number of inhabited houses had scarcely grown at all in the half-century. Parish rate books show that many houses were divided into two, three or four tenements. The proportion of inhabitants to houses was highest in the central parts of the town, and there was very little extension of the house-area in the outer parishes.

The latter half of the eighteenth century witnessed a phenomenal growth of the industrial towns of the northern counties and midlands of England, and the census of 1801 showed that the population of the whole of England had increased during the last two decades by more than 20 per cent. The comparative stagnation of Cambridge was due to some obvious causes. The town had no native industries: the trade in wool had deserted it for other parts. Sturbridge Fair, which from tolls and incidentals had once been a source of much profit, was fallen into great decay: the procession of the Corporation at its opening was given up in 1790. Of the well-to-do country gentry, who used to get their supplies from Cambridge tradesmen, many left the county, and between 1780 and 1800 many old manor houses were pulled down. Worst of all, there had been a great and continuous falling off since 1700 in the number of University residents. The proportion of non-residents among fellows of colleges had much increased and the numbers of the undergraduates had been much reduced.

Though the town population had increased, the area occupied by houses was much the same as in the days of Elizabeth.[1] A New Plan of Cambridge as it was in

[1] Custance's Plan marks *Spittle End* and *Castle End* as the extreme north and south limits of Cambridge; curiously enough, in the old play, *Gammer Gurton's Needle*, acted at Christ's College about 1563, 'the spittle house' and 'castel's end' are spoken of as the Dan and Beersheba of the town of the supposed scene.

1798 was made by William Custance, a local builder and surveyor. It shows that in Trumpington Street the houses reached barely as far as Spittle End, *i.e.* the corner of Lensfield Road: on the Hills road to the near corner of Parker's Piece: in Jesus Lane to the Fellow's Garden of Jesus College. Except for a few cottages near Magdalene College there were no dwellings in Chesterton Lane until Chesterton village was reached. At the Castle End the house line extended as far as Pleasant Row. On the St Neots Road there was not a single habitation, nor any on the western side of the river, except a few congregated in Newnham suburb. From Barnwell village to the wall of Christ's College garden, there was open field. St Thomas' Leys stretched as far as Downing Street, and Coe Fen Leys to the site of St Peter's Terrace. Though since 1800 the inhabited area has been trebled or quadrupled, it is well to remember that Cambridge is still to an appreciable extent a rural township, and that within its boundaries it includes arable and pasture lands reaching nearly to Girton College, to the by-way that quits the St Neots Road for Madingley village, and to the Binn Brook crossing of the Barton Road. In 1800 a walk of five to ten minutes in any direction would bring the town-dweller from the Market Place to the open field, which was still Cambridge; and in most directions it would take him at least half an hour to arrive at a spot where he crossed a boundary into land that was not Cambridge.

The Cambridge that was dwelt in might be likened to a cottage in a very large garden—perhaps more aptly to a kernel contained in a thick and hard shell. To crack the shell was the problem. The cultivators of the garden were many and not easily to be displaced. By purchase or otherwise they had acquired the use of their strips; but they could scarcely be regarded as freeholders. In their occupation of the soil they were strictly limited by immemorial and immutable custom, against which Law could enter no plea. Each must cultivate his holding after a rule prescribed by primitive usage, and in such manner as should be least detrimental to other cultivators in the Field, if also with least advantage to Cambridge town. Anything of the nature of encroachment, whether by private individuals or corporations, was a breach of Field Custom, and the building of permanent dwellings on the Field was effectually an encroachment. With the rights of the strip-holders the Town never attempted to interfere: but sometimes they cast covetous eyes on the pasture, which was common to a variety of individuals. In 1579 and in 1627 the Corporation propose to enclose and let Jesus Green for a limited time, employing the profits for the relief of the poor. In 1667 they want to erect pesthouses on Coldham's Common; it can only be done by Act of Parliament, and the commoners object. The Corporation may pass regulations for the use of the common pasture, but it draws no rents from the arable field and clearly has no ownership. There is talk of ancient 'manors' in the Field— Merton College, the Hospital of St John, the Nuns of St Radegund, &c.—but the supposed lords hold no courts, and the tenants owe no manorial service and hold under no law of copyhold. Possibly—though the evidence is lacking—the King, when he granted the town in farm to the burgesses, did not part with his property in the soil. So to the King and his Parliament the Corporation must go, if they would extinguish— of course with compensation to individuals—the vexatious and wasteful Custom of the Field.

Enclosure, arbitrary and unsanctioned by Parliament, was common enough in Tudor days. The business was much accelerated by legislation after 1760, and before the end of the century upwards of 1800 enclosing Acts had been passed. In 1801 an Act was passed for extinguishing the commoners' rights in the lands called St Thomas' Leys, which were wanted as a site for Downing College. Next year an Act was obtained for enclosing the Field, known as Cambridge Field, on the northern and western sides of the town. In 1807 another Act was passed for enclosing Barnwell Field, containing 1156 acres, and in 1811 another for enclosing Coe Fen Leys, where the Leys School now stands. A plan of the town dated 1842, when the population was about 24,000, but before the railway had reached Cambridge, shows that the inhabited area had then extended far into the Field, especially on the southern and eastern sides of the town. A New Town, as it was called, had sprung up between Christ's and Parker's Pieces and the formerly isolated village of Barnwell. Regent Street and Coronation Street in their names tell of a period which witnessed the extension of the town streets about the Hills Road. Mill Road takes its name from a windmill which stood in Barnwell Field at the S.E. corner of Parker's Piece; Fitzroy Street from George Henry Fitzroy, Duke of Grafton, who was M.P. for the University at the date of the enclosure; and Burleigh Street from a patriotic Cambridge carrier who in 1798 furnished horses and waggons for military service. In the forty years ending 1841 the population of St Andrew's the Less parish, Barnwell, increased from 252 to 9486, a larger number than was contained in the whole of Cambridge in 1801.

M

CHAPTER XIX

The Downfall of the Old Corporation

THE Eagle (now bereft of the Child) is in these years of grace an inn of a modest reputation; at its temperate refections I am unaware that the Mayor and Common Council are entertained by any anonymous benefactor. Yet about it memories cling of robuster convivialities, and, adopting Keats' apostrophe to the Mermaid Tavern, we may imagine that souls of Aldermen dead and gone—if souls they had, or have—hover regretfully about the old house where they 'supped and bowsed' in the grand epoch of the Rutland Club. With a corresponding melancholy the present writer has now to record how the flood came and there was an end of eating and drinking.

To realise that in Cambridge town such things were, scarcely a century ago, requires a somewhat resolute imagination. 'Bowsing' was, no doubt, the special efflorescence of the Georgian age, but the conditions began with King John. When that monarch made a composition with the burgesses of Cambridge he was chiefly concerned in driving a bargain with them which should satisfy his need of cash, while dispensing with the intervention of a middle-man in the person of the sheriff who deducted his 'third penny' from the sum of borough dues for which he accounted to the royal exchequer. He did not ask who were the burgesses —whether all, or only some, of the inhabitants— and in conferring on them the privilege of 'holding' the town he did not specify any duties to which they should be liable for the betterment of the community among whom they dwelt. When a Councilman told the Municipal Commissioners in 1833 that he thought

that corporate property belonged *bona fide* to the
Corporation, to do with it as they were pleased, some
of his fellow Councillors professed to be shocked at
the bold assertion of a principle on which, nevertheless,
they had always acted. Perhaps the speaker had the
support of law and usage. Charters recognise burgesses :
of the townsmen who are not burgesses they take no
note. In days when kings could, and did, revoke
charters there was always a chance that considerations
of public advantage would outweigh the interest of
local bureaucrats. Time was when the University,
with the Privy Council behind it, was vigilant in
demanding that the Town authorities should do this or
that to its satisfaction, and, if 'bailies' overstepped the
law, hedge-breaking provided a rough remedy. Those
days were gone. The Glorious Revolution, with its
brave declaration of liberty and right, had firmly
established the rule of oligarchs.

Consuetudines, 'the free customs which they had
in the time of their ancestors'—what were these which
King John granted to the burgesses? That was the
question debated at length in the King's Bench in a
suit brought by the Corporation against certain unfree
inhabitants of Cambridge in the year 1829. Custom
is a thing fluid and forgettable; it lives in the interpretation of the time. Are there any elements in
borough custom that are prescriptive, constant and
indisputable? There are the old landgable and hagable, payments originally made to the king's exchequer
for certain houses and lands in the borough : there are
similar payments for lands once 'waste' but later
'approved,' *i.e.* enclosed by license : there are certain
market tolls and profits of fairs, assigned to the burgesses
by royal writings. These items made up a very
modest total—little more than £600 by the year.
No doubt there had been a great falling off in the
once lucrative business of the fairs. The Corporation
might fairly plead that the tenuity of their revenue

absolved them from undertaking any large scheme for the benefit of the town. It had always been so. From the days of Edward I a succession of Acts of Parliament had been passed to enable the Mayor and Bailiffs, in aid of the paving of the town, to take tolls of various articles of merchandise brought to the town for sale; but in all cases the license was only for a short term of years. In 1788 an Act was obtained 'for the better paving, cleansing and lighting of the town, removing obstructions and widening the streets.' In place of the bailiffs, who in former Acts were charged with collecting the tolls and carrying out the work, certain Commissioners representing the Town, County and University were appointed to put the Act in execution, and of the expenses two-fifths were to be defrayed by the University and the residue was to be raised by certain rates and tolls. The yearly sum expended by the Commissioners ranged from £3000 to £5000, and to the total the Corporation, which from this time did nothing for street repairs, contributed no more than £10 per annum. The 'improvements' carried out by the Corporation were of the most trivial kind. In 1818 they 'built' Garret Hostel Bridge, a wooden structure, and paid the contractor £330, but the work was so badly done that it had to be 'rebuilt' three years later for a further £140. In 1835 the Corporation was indicted for not repairing this unlucky bridge, and having no funds to defend the action, allowed judgment to be entered against it by default.

For some time before the passing of the Act of 1788, the Corporation had been exacting tolls of all persons, not being freemen, who brought loaded carts into the town, and afterwards the same toll had been levied on carts going out laden. Until recent years there still remained a board fixed to the wall of Queens' College, next the town bridge, whereon the scale of tolls was set forth. The charge for every laden cart was twopence. The Corporation claimed a prescriptive right to the toll because of their repairs to Garret Hostel Bridge, the Small Bridges and the Market Hill. Since 1743 it was the custom of the Corporation to lease all its tolls for certain terms of years to individuals who appointed the collectors. During the last half of the eighteenth century the average of the annual payments by the lessees was about £230. After 1800, partly, no doubt, in consequence of increasing trade, but more because of a stricter exaction, the amount was much larger, and in 1822 was £750. The collectors stood generally at the chief entrances to the town, and marked with chalk each cart that had paid its twopence : but carters might be called on to pay in any street of the town. Women and girls were often employed to collect : one old lady who hobbled with a stick stationed herself in Silver Street and dropped her takings in a pitcher. Often payment was refused. One toller, having been thrashed by a carter, summoned him for assault and payment : the Alderman who heard the case ordered the carter to pay, and when he refused to do so, thought it wiser to let the matter drop.

The imposition of this duty for an unlimited time and without Parliamentary sanction was much resented by the Cambridge public, and their dissatisfaction with the arbitrary doings of their rulers was sharply edged when they were rated by the Commissioners for effective improvements and at the same time were charged by the Corporation for neglecting their office. As early as 1786 an action was instituted against one of the collectors for taking distress for non-payment of the cart tolls. Nothing came of it, and the matter rested until 1824.

In that year several inhabitants of the town resolved to have the issue tried and started a subscription to defray the costs of legal proceedings against the Corporation. The cart toll was resisted, and in consequence the Corporation brought actions against three trading firms of Cambridge, the principal of which was that of

Messrs Beales, who were dealers in corn and coals. Their carts went out to all parts of the country and neighbourhood, and they had a large trade at the port of Lynn. Mr S. P. Beales, the leading partner and chief defendant in the action, was scarcely a disinterested Hampden. He had built for himself a dwelling house at the place in Newnham called the Armitage (Hermitage), which he had bought from the Corporation for a nominal sum, and adjoining it his firm had a quay, granary and warehouse. As Cambridge freemen were exempted from toll for the use of the port of Lynn, Beales applied to one of the Mortlock family to be admitted to the freedom, offering to pay £100 for the privilege; but as he declined to support Rutland candidates he failed in his request.

The action against Messrs Beales was tried in January, 1826, at Westminster Hall, and a verdict was found for the defendants, but the rule was suspended pending the result of another action against the firm of Fisher and Son. This second action was tried in December, 1827, when a verdict was found for the Corporation. The action against Messrs Beales was tried again in December, 1829, and again a verdict was given for the defendants. Though the Corporation applied for a new trial it was refused by the Court, and the inhabitants of Cambridge were thus finally exonerated from the payment of the Corporation toll.

The result was simply calamitous to the Corporation. During the protracted proceedings they had been unable to exact the toll, and the verdict deprived them of half their income. Their legal charges amounted to more than £4000, and the cost to the defendants to as much more. The Rutland Club was irrevocably routed and disappeared. A contemporary journal says:

'The leading members of the Corporation have been in the constant habit of dining together on the evening or afternoon preceding the assizes and inviting their friends at the expense of the body corporate, but owing to their pecuniary difficulties the

THE MARKET PLACE IN 1842

table no longer groans beneath substantial cheer or the flowing bowls of Bacchus, but presented the *uncivic* appearance of a tea equipage.   The feast, as might be expected, was much less joyously attended, nor were they so jocund, but their demeanour was of course perfectly correct.'

For the liquidation of their debt the Corporation found a stalwart friend in one of the town members, Colonel Trench, on whose introduction another M.P., Mr Leak, lent them £3000 at 3½ per cent. interest. With sad gratitude and a boding that their voice was to be stilled by Reform they re-elected Colonel Trench to represent the burgesses in 1829.

It was the last occasion of a Parliamentary election by the old constituency.   Already the engine of Reform was at the door and ready to smite.   In April 1820 a large meeting of the borough inhabitants was held at the Shire Hall—the Mayor having refused to convene it— at which resolutions were passed denouncing the corrupt system by which, through the secret and unconstitutional influence of a noble family, the inhabitants were excluded from the administration of town affairs and from the power to vote in the election of representatives of the borough.   Similar meetings of county freeholders were convened by the Sheriff in 1821 and 1822.   By the Reform Act (1832) the constituency was greatly enlarged by the admission to the franchise of all £10 householders, and freemen who did not reside within seven miles from the borough were disfranchised. At the election of 1832 under the new conditions of the franchise the voters were 1247: at the last contested election under the old system the votes delivered were less than thirty.

The Act of 1832 was the passing bell of the old Corporation.   But it was not dead yet, and, unsupported by the enfranchised householders, for a few years longer it kept up a desultory retiring action against the invaders of its privileges.   In August 1833 forty-one freemen were elected, all of them Tories.   In

February 1834 the Corporation joined with corporations of other towns in resolutions to use all constitutional means to defeat the design of wresting from them their ancient liberties. In July 1835 counter petitions were addressed to the House of Lords, by the inhabitants and by the Corporation, for and against the Municipal Corporations Bill.

In October and November 1833 two of the Commissioners for enquiring into the state of Municipal Corporations held a public Court at the Guildhall. They inspected charters and the books of the Corporation and examined thirty-two witnesses, of whom nineteen were connected with the Corporation. The evidence offered was, to say the least, surprising. The general facts were as follows:

The freedom of the borough was conferred by the Mayor, Bailiffs and Burgesses, and they, by the selective method described on p. 45, chose the Mayor and all officers. The body of the freemen voted on one side, and none of the minority were ever selected to choose the Mayor. Freedom could be obtained by birth, apprenticeship, purchase or gift: on an average about one was admitted each year on the first two of these qualifications; between forty and fifty tradesmen were freemen by purchase. There were 118 resident and forty non-resident freemen; twenty of the latter who were admitted in 1788 were tenants of the Duke of Rutland at Cheveley or Belvoir. The Duke was elected High Steward in 1818, and his brother was Recorder. Aldermen were elected for life, and residence in the borough was not required of them: four of the twelve were non-resident.

For the policing of the town there were a High Constable, a Chief Constable, a Serjeant at Mace, and six watchmen. There were fifty-one parish constables, mostly tradesmen: they had no regular wage, but received about four shillings for each warrant. When special constables were required they were chosen exclusively from the Tory side. At the last election General Manners was wounded, and the special constables were disarmed and put to flight.

In 1832 the Corporation income from rents, leases and tolls amounted to £944: the lost street tolls would have brought in £750 more. In the last fourteen years the Corporation had expended £7569 in actions at law, and between £500 and £600 for the benefit of the town. It had been paying off debt all those years and had had advances of money from Mr Mortlock. A sum of £1500, which was not accounted for, had been paid to Mr Butcher, a solicitor introduced by the Mortlocks. Mr Butcher was reported to have said, ' I would vote against my conscience if I could get anything by it. Damn conscience—what's conscience to me?'

The rule of the Mortlocks, one alderman affirmed, was very bad. If the Corporation had not sold its property it would have had an income of £2000 for the improvement of the town. An alderman had purchased for two guineas a building site valued at from £100 to £120: sales to the Mortlock family were equally discreditable.

There had been a wholesale misappropriation of Trust Funds. Many charitable bequests had lapsed, and the income was not accounted for. Crane's charity, which since 1658 had brought to the Corporation, as trustees, £492 in every fifth year, ' had gone to sleep, and never waked.' A freeman alleged that the Corporation had not paid his bill, on the ground that they were waiting until they received the charity money. Another charity was that of Sir Thomas White (1566) which, once in every twenty-four years, brought to the Corporation £104 for making loans to freemen. Until 1763 it had been so applied, but since then, until 1808, no account had been kept of it, and no loans had been made. In 1811 the latest payment of £104 had been made to the Mayor, Mr Mortlock, who kept it in his hands until 1828, and then advanced loans amounting to £100. In 1834 an action was brought against the Corporation for maladministration of the trust, and they were condemned to refund the sum of £1086, and also pay costs to the informer amounting to £224.

It was held by the Corporation that it was not their business to look after the town commons, which contained 310 acres. Rights of pasture had formerly belonged only to occupants of tenements 'which from old time had been used as dwelling-houses': now the commons were open to all inhabitants. They were in a filthy, undrained state. 'If the Mayor,' who lived opposite Midsummer Common, 'had not had a hardy constitution he would have died of *cholera morbus*.' Cattle were dragged with difficulty out of the mud at Coe Fen.

Chapter XX.

Freedom and Independence

By the Municipal Corporations Act of 1835 the old Corporation of 'the Mayor, Bailiffs and Burgesses' was dissolved and a new Corporation styled 'the Mayor, Aldermen and Burgesses' was erected in its place. All male occupiers of houses, counting-houses, shops or warehouses rated at £10, who were habitant within the borough or within seven miles of it, were constituted burgesses and members of the corporate body. The governing power was vested in a Council consisting of ten Aldermen and thirty Councillors, by and from among whom the Mayor was to be chosen annually. The borough was divided into five wards, each having an allotted number of Councillors chosen by the burgesses of the ward. One third of the Councillors of each ward was to go out of office annually, and one half of the Aldermen every three years. Clauses were added enacting that nothing in the Act should affect the rights and privileges of the University, exempting its members from compulsion to serve in any office in or under the corporate body and from being charged with any rate which by law could not be levied on them, and providing that the occupation of premises in any College or Hall should not entitle any person to be enrolled as a burgess. The first elections to the new Council took place in December, 1835, and resulted in a sweeping majority for the reforming party.

In March of the following year the Poor Law Commissioners made an Order that for the administration of the Poor Law the fourteen parishes of the town should be united under the control of Guardians elected

179

by the parishes. About the same time the Watch Committee created under the provisions of the Municipal Corporations Act established a police force consisting of a superintendent, two inspectors, four serjeants, and twenty-four constables.

The first act of the new Council was to remove the Duke of Rutland from the office of High Steward, and his brother from the Recordership: in the Duke's place they chose Francis, Lord Godolphin. Thomas Hovell, who had taken a principal part in Corporation reform, was elected Mayor. The flood of reform which swept away so much that was old and corrupt, threatened to carry off some things old and not necessarily corrupt. The Corporation plate, china, glass and table-linen were sold for £133: some of the plate was old and valuable. It was even proposed to sell the silver maces, five in number and splendid for weight and workmanship: but this was not agreed to. A much more questionable measure, approved by the Council in 1841, but fortunately dropped owing to the opposition which it evoked in the town, was to enclose portions of the commons and dispose of the land for building sites and market gardens. With very little evidence to support them the Corporation claimed—as the old Corporation had never done—'an undoubted property in the soil, as lords of the manor.'

Even before the dissolution of the unreformed Corporation, but not on its initiative, gas-lighting had come to Cambridge. The streets were first lighted with oil-gas in 1823. In London a Company for the supply of coal-gas was formed in 1810. Soon after 1823 John Grafton opened gas retorts in Gas Lane, Barnwell, and contracted with the Commissioners to light the streets with 'inflammable air or gas obtained from coal.' In 1834 a Company was started to take over his business, and Parliamentary powers were obtained for the purpose in that year. The public supply of water waited until 1853, when the Cambridge

University and Town Waterworks Company was incorporated. Hitherto the methods of extinguishing fire had remained pretty much as they have been described in Chapter XVII. At a disastrous fire, in 1849, which destroyed eight houses between Great St Mary's church and the Market Hill, such water as could be got to extinguish it was obtained either from Hobson's Conduit or the river at Garret Hostel Bridge.

The clearance made by this fire had a notable result. Before 1849 the chancel of Great St Mary's church was hidden behind a row of small houses which reached from St Mary's Street to St Mary's Passage, and formed one side of a lane, variously called Pump Lane or Warwick Street. 'The original Market Hill,' says Mr A. B. Gray, 'was little more than a wide street between Market Street and Petty Cury, whilst at right angles to it lay a somewhat larger area connecting Petty Cury with the northern end of Peas Hill, and known as Market Ward. The rest of the square was occupied by a large block of irregular houses clustered together like a rookery, extending as far south as the present railings in St Mary's Passage, and nearly as far east as Rose Crescent, whilst its western part overflowed into St Mary's churchyard, so that, it has been gravely stated, worshippers within could obtain an excellent view of the interior of an adjoining bedroom.' The eastern limb of this L-shaped Market Place was faced by the Town Hall, in front of which stood the so-called Hobson's Conduit. Market stalls also occupied Peas Hill, as they do at present, but opposite the east end of St Edward's church there was an island block of low houses which made the open space narrower than it is now ; the last of them were not removed until 1874. Until 1842 the Cattle Market had been held on St Andrew's Hill, otherwise 'the Hog Market,' but in that year it was removed to Pound Hill, at the Castle End. In the last quarter of the nineteenth century it travelled to the ample site between the

Railway and the Cherryhinton Road. The Hay Market, which had been held near St Clement's church, was removed in 1820 to a piece of ground near Pound Hill. The old Corn Exchange on St Andrew's Hill was opened in 1842; formerly the Corn Market was at the north end of the Market Place, opposite the Rose Inn. The present Corn Exchange was completed in 1875.

The fire of 1849 gave Cambridge a market-place worthy of its dignity and consequence in trade. Other 'improvements' of about the same date redeemed the town from the reproach of medieval constriction and rusticity, if at the same time they effaced some things that were medieval and picturesque. Of such changes a correspondent of the *Cambridge Portfolio* writes with the enthusiasm characteristic of 1840. The traveller by the 'Rocket' coach who enters Cambridge by Trumpington Street will be told that:

> improvement is marked out for Peterhouse, and Pembroke is going to build, and will wish himself years younger for the chance of seeing these dreams of futurity fulfilled. Many are the mean structures that have given place to the Pitt Press. The eye, once confined by the narrow line of low habitations, over which towered the pinnacles of King's College, as if they belonged to another world, now ranges over a wide expanse of architectural richness and perspective effect. Where now is the breadth that fulfils the modern notion of street propriety, not more than twelve years ago was the narrowest of the narrow streets of Cambridge, wherein the foot passenger walked as it were beneath the first floors of the houses, and their walls formed the street border.

And yet, with all its inconveniences of narrow alleys, dripping eaves and uncensored laystalls there remain some lovers of antiquity who are disposed to think of old Cambridge as William Harrison wrote of it in 1577. 'For uniformitie of building, orderlie compaction and politike regiment the towne of Cambridge, as the newer workmanship, exceedeth that of Oxford by manie a fold.'

The old Town Gaol, described in Chapter XVII,

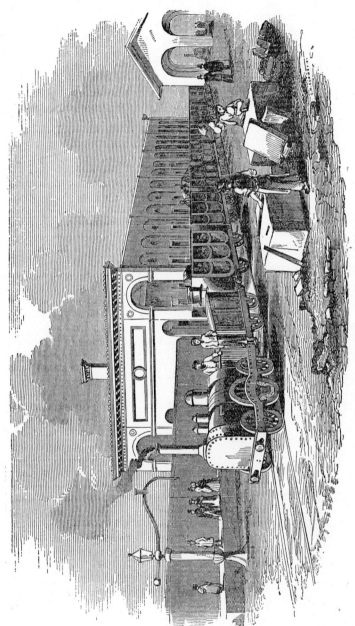

CAMBRIDGE RAILWAY STATION IN 1847

had been removed in 1790, and a new one was built at the back of Hobson's Workhouse, commonly known as the Spinning House. The cost of the building was only £991. In its time-dishonoured squalor the old building had served its purpose for five centuries and a half: its successor lasted only for a generation. In 1827 an Act was passed for building a new prison. It was erected on a piece of ground 'on the outskirts of the town,' on the south side of Parker's Piece, where Queen Anne Terrace now stands. It cost the extravagant sum of £25,000, which was raised by a special rate. It was removed in 1878, and prisoners were afterwards committed to the County Gaol at the Castle End until that, in its turn, was disused for the purpose.

Between 1782 and 1812 many proposals were ventilated for connecting the Cam at Cambridge with the Thames by a canal starting from the Stort at Bishop Stortford and proceeding by way of Saffron Walden. These schemes were promoted by the Navigation Committee of London and were opposed by the Corporation of Cambridge, the Bedford Level Corporation and various landowners, and nothing resulted. The first proposal of a railway connecting Cambridge with London was made in 1825 by a company called the London Northern Railroad Company. Nothing came of this and several other schemes for lines passing through Cambridge to Manchester and York which were proposed between 1834 and 1841. In 1842 assent was given to an Act to enable the Eastern Counties Railway Company to construct a railway from the Northern and Eastern Railway at Newport to Cambridge and thence eastward to Brandon and westward to Peterborough. The University authorities were not a little apprehensive of the evil communications to which their pupils would be exposed by such immediate contact with the outer and, consequently, unhallowed world, and they took precautions accordingly. They contrived to exorcise the devil by exiling the Station to an inconvenient distance from the centre of the town and the innocent surroundings of green fields. They also got clauses inserted in the Act empowering the officers of the University to have free access to all parts of the Depôt or Station at the time of starting or arriving of trains, and to demand and have from the servants of the Company information with reference to any person being or suspected to be a person *in statu pupillari*, and further to require that the Company should refuse to convey any such person, though he might have paid his fare, if he should have been identified to a servant of the Company and warning should have been given of his intention to travel upon the line : and that the Company should forfeit five pounds in the case of each passenger conveyed after such warning. In 1851 a reverend Vice-Chancellor in a letter addressed to the Directors expressed his pain that they ' had made arrangements for conveying foreigners and others to Cambridge at such fares as might be likely to tempt persons who, having no regard for Sunday themselves, would inflict their presence on the University on that day of rest ' ; and, as the interpreter of the Divine as well as the academic mind, he pointed out that ' the contemplated arrangements were as distasteful to the University authorities as they must be offensive to Almighty God and to all right-minded Christians.'

With the advent of the railway abruptly ended the epoch of the Stage-coach. For a few years longer some local coaches held the roads; that which ran between Cambridge and Bedford survived until 1849. Tom Henesey, once the dandy driver of the Stamford ' Regent ' on the York road, ended his days as the driver of a two-horse 'bus between Cambridge and Huntingdon.

The perfectibility of the elector, which had been anticipated by the authors of the first Reform Act, did not, in the case of Cambridge, by any means result in any shadow of perfection until a generation at least

N

had passed away since 1832. The outcome of the Act was the transference of the franchise from a small, corrupt, but comparatively educated clique of freemen to a much larger body, of which the preponderating element was much more ignorant and not less corrupt than the followers of the Rutland drum had been— so corrupt indeed that the Rutlands regained the representation of the borough as soon as the electors discovered that Rutlands were more liberal than Whigs, though it may be said of the Whigs that, lacking funds, they lacked not the generous instinct.

In 1853 a Royal Commission, appointed to examine into corrupt practices at Parliamentary elections for the borough, examined 298 witnesses and issued a highly instructive report respecting all the elections from 1839 to 1852 inclusive.

The evidence showed that in 1785 Mr Mortlock, who then possessed absolutely the power of returning members, sold his influence, as it was said, for a large sum of money to the then Duke of Rutland. Elections, then and until 1832, 'were conducted in a quiet, inexpensive manner, almost resembling a domestic transaction.' As applied to those elections, 'quiet' seems a curiously chosen epithet, and the Duke of Rutland best knew whether they were inexpensive. The Reform Act created a constituency which in 1852 consisted of 1850 householders, 28 freemen who were also householders, and only nine pure freemen. Parties were about equally divided, and corruption was practised by both of them. Apart from direct bribery it consisted in employing very large numbers of persons to act as flag-bearers, messengers, &c., who were recommended for employment by electors, and received extravagant wages, the total sum amounting to half the cost of an election.

Between 1839 and 1852 there had been seven Parliamentary elections. In 1841 the chances of the Tory candidate were considered to be so poor that

neither party had resorted to direct bribery; in all the
other contests there was clear evidence of systematic
and widespread bribery. Candidates paid their
charges, usually amounting to about £1000 each,
without enquiry as to the disposal of their money,
and of course professed to have no suspicion of its
corrupt employment. The Bribery Act was a dead
letter and had no deterrent effect. It was usual to
import agents from Norwich 'celebrated for their
ingenuity in electioneering matters'; but Cambridge
also had its own Abanas of corruption, familiar to all
men as Hobson's conduit and as universal in their lavish-
ment. The method of one such agent, Samuel Long,
was to inspect the rate books and find who was in
arrears, and once bribed a voter was bribeable ever
after. 'A conventional language was established in
which communications passed between Long and the
voters: it was his practice to tell a voter to *go and do
what was right* and *he would do what was right.*' Otherwise it was enough to look at the voter 'in a peculiar
manner,' or leave a message with his wife that 'Long
had called.' The day after the voting a parcel, un-
addressed, was left at the voter's door, containing
money. Electors who had been promised £5 by the
Whigs voted Tory for £10. In 1839 Long was
convicted and imprisoned for bribery—and received
£200 in compensation. At the election of 1843 he
was dogged all day by an agent of the opposite party
in order to watch his proceedings; but, as he assured the
Commissioners, 'it made no difference: he could bribe
just as well before his face as behind his back.' In
1845 the poll was going ill for the Tory, when within
the last hour a majority was suddenly obtained for
him.

> 'A number of voters were assembled at a public-house, the Star
> and Garter, and refused to vote unless money was paid down to
> them. Some time elapsed before anything was done. At last
> Long was despatched to secure their votes. He took with him
> money and a man named Stearne; this man he posted in a room

where was a window with part of a pane out, and the blind down. The names of the voters were called, one by one, and the assistant was supplied with a sum of money (£10 in all instances, save one, where it was £12). This he handed out to each individual as he came forward. The hand came out through the hole in the window; no other part of the person was seen. Some were bribed at so late an hour that, though they ran all the way, they did not arrive in time to vote.'

In 1852 a calumnious report went about that Long had been promised 'a hatful of money' if he would transfer his allegiance to the Whigs, but he 'satisfactorily explained' that his acquaintance with their candidate was limited to the remark, 'It is a fine afternoon'; however, in the cryptic language used at election time a casual expression might be significant of much.

The evidence obtained by the Commissioners showed that a large proportion of the electorate had no education to fit them for the exercise of the franchise. Very many of the bribed electors were unable to write their names. At Cambridge, as elsewhere, there was no time so miserably equipped as the first half of the nineteenth century for the education of the middle and lower classes. The Perse School was in prolonged swoon; in 1844 hardly twenty boys were taught there. A meagre education was given to children of the poorer class in the Charity, i.e. Church of England, schools. As originally provided in 1703 the number was 260; in 1796 it had grown to 418, but for lack of funds was then reduced to 300, and so it continued until 1842, though the population of the town had quadrupled since 1703. As recently as 1866 the children attending these schools numbered 1663, and the ordinary expenditure was less than £900 per annum. A British, i.e. non-sectarian, School was opened in 1840, and in 1850 an Industrial School, which owed its origin mainly to Dr Harvey Goodwin, afterwards Bishop of Carlisle, was started in Victoria Road, Chesterton: it is now the Home for Waifs and Strays.

Chapter XXI.

Greater Cambridge

In the twenty years between 1831 and 1851 the population of Cambridge increased from 20,917 to 27,803. The ratio of increase was somewhat less than that of England and Wales, as a whole, in the same period, but, as Cambridge has no mining district adjoining, nor any manufacturing opportunities, it is sufficiently remarkable. By the enclosure of the common fields it had been possible greatly to extend the formerly confined area of habitation. Railway communication in 1851 was still in its infancy, and as yet had done little to promote the commercial prosperity of the town. But improved methods of drainage, the intensive cultivation which had been generally introduced since 1836, and the high prices prevailing for agricultural produce had added greatly to the wealth of the Eastern Counties, and particularly of Cambridge town, as is evidenced by the attention paid by the Corporation at this time to the borough markets. What small industrial consequence the town had once possessed completely deserted it before 1800, but as an emporium it won a novel importance.

The contribution of the University to this augmented prosperity was of small account. Compared with its growth in the years which preceded and followed this period the advance of the University was singularly insignificant. Matriculations, which had been 105 in 1801, rose to 315 in 1831, and to no more than 355 in 1851. Energy in all branches of municipal life had been the outcome of the reforms of 1832 and 1835. The University fenced itself within the limits of its Elizabethan constitution, and from those ramparts flew

the banners of exclusive Anglicanism. No longer
was the old war of privilege waged with an obscure
lot of self-appointed bailiffs and councillors : the chosen
representatives of some thousands of independent
citizens were not people to submit themselves and the
electors to the suzerainty which the University had held
and exercised for some six centuries.

In 1842 ' a new and handsome Shire House ' (Cooper)
was completed after the designs of John Howard, the
philanthropist.   To make way for it ' the spacious
and massive Gatehouse, the sole relic of the Castle,'
was removed.   The old Shirehouse, ' a most incom-
modious building,' was put up in 1747 and stood in
front of the Guildhall, on a site leased to the County
at a peppercorn rent for 999 years.   It formed, in
fact, the front of the present Guildhall, and was built
on arches, so that the space beneath might be used for
market stalls.   As the Castle was not within the borough
limits the Shire House and its satellite Gaol found an
appropriate place on County ground, where Picot,
the sheriff, had executed rude justice in the days of
the Conqueror.

Of incidents deserving record in the faithful *Annals*
of Cooper the early years of Victoria's reign supply
variety and abundance : of events worthy of the white
mark of History there are practically none.   The progress of the Town was like the growth of summer grass,
' unseen, but crescive in its faculty.'   Partly from the
concession of municipal powers under the Act of 1835,
more from the native consciousness of its citizens,
Cambridge Town arrived at a due sense of its importance and independence of the leading-strings which
for centuries had tied it to its ' unjust stepmother,'
the Alma Mater of the scholars.   The University, on
the other hand, by neglecting to exercise its privileges,
tacitly admitted that the age of privilege had passed.
In the years 1852–1860 it was much more concerned
in harmonising its own outworn statutes with the

requirements of the developed studies of the day than with old quarrels with its neighbours which had lost their significance and lent nothing to its dignity.

In 1855 the matters in difference between the University and the Town were submitted to the arbitration of Sir John Patteson, formerly a judge in the court of King's Bench. In marked contrast with the bitterness evoked in similar controversy in past times the questions in issue were presented in the most amicable form, and the University was well content to leave matters which had formerly been regarded as of vital importance to the decision of the arbitrator. The result of the inquiry was the very important 'Cambridge Award Act' of 1856. The main points in this Act were the following:

1. The oaths and declarations of the Mayor, aldermen and others to conserve the liberties and privileges of the University were abolished.

2. The power of the Vice-Chancellor to grant alehouse licenses was abrogated, and though the power of granting wine licenses was retained to him, no sum should be taken by the University from the persons licensed.[1]

3. The authority of supervising weights and measures was transferred from the University to the justices of peace for the borough, and the powers exercised by the University officers with respect to markets and fairs were withdrawn.

4. The right of the University to claim 'conusance' in actions at law wherein a member of the University was a party was to cease.

5. The property of the University and of the Colleges, with certain exceptions, was to be assessed to rates, as other property in the borough, the valuation being determined by three valuers,

---

[1] The power of granting wine licenses is still retained by the University—the sole relic of its ancient control of the sale of provisions and liquors.

two of them appointed severally by the Vice-Chancellor and the Mayor, and the third appointed by the other two jointly as umpire, before proceeding to valuation.

6. The Watch Committee was to consist of fifteen members, *viz.*, the Mayor and nine members of the Council together with five appointed by the University.

7. The borough accounts were to be audited annually by three members of the University and three of the Town.

8. The sum contributed by the University for the purposes of the Improvement Commission was reduced from two-fifths to one quarter of the whole.

On the other hand the privileges of the University were retained in the following matters.

1. The power of the Vice-Chancellor to prohibit theatrical and other entertainments except in Long Vacation.

2. The power of discommoning (with certain limitations).

3. The powers exercised by the proctors.

In the same year the University passed graces relinquishing its right to license victuallers in Chesterton and discontinuing the office of Taxor. As a signal mark of the amicable relations existing between them the University and the Town combined to present ' a handsome silver candelabrum of the value of 300 guineas ' to Sir John Patteson ' in grateful acknowledgement of his services as arbitrator.'

Of the few relics of the privileges reserved to it by the Award Act the University presently willingly divested itself. The old House of Correction, established by Hobson, the carrier, and governed by trustees appointed by the University and the Town, owing to a decision of Lord Langdale, Master of the Rolls, in 1837, had ceased to be used as a Workhouse, and its employment for the imprisonment of petty offenders ended in 1790, when the new Gaol was built at the back of it. For many years it had been used solely— and that seldom—for the confinement of ' common women.' In that matter the Proctors had the power of arrest and the Vice-Chancellor that of committing to the Spinning House, as it was called. In consequence of a misapplication of this power in one case considerable feeling was aroused among the townsmen, and as a result of amicable negotiations between the Borough Council and the University the rights of the latter were surrendered to the civil authorities by an Act of Parliament of 1894.

In the same year the University relinquished its ban on unlicensed dramatic and other entertainments. Before then stage performances and even public concerts, except in Long Vacation, had to be licensed by the Vice-Chancellor and the Mayor, and they usually took place in the Guildhall. In that year, principally on the initiation of Mr W. B. Redfern, afterwards Mayor, and of Mr J. W. Clark, afterwards University Registrary, a disused skating rink, opposite the Police Station, was adapted for theatrical use, and received the name of St Andrew's Hall. On the same site the present New Theatre was built in 1895, and opened by Mr and Mrs Beerbohm Tree and the London Haymarket Company with a performance of *Hamlet*, in January, 1896. The old Barnwell Theatre ' lagged superfluous' until 1878, when it was sold and converted into a Mission Hall. It was built by Wilkins, the architect of the new buildings at King's and Corpus, who had a private box in it, which he used to lend to ' dons ' and ladies in its summer season. To judge from the seating it was a house of little ease. Such prosperity as it ever had waned with the waning of Sturbridge Fair.

In 1853 it was decided by a vote taken of the rate-payers to adopt the Act for establishing a Borough Library. Two years later a Reference Library was opened in the then disused Quaker meeting house in Jesus Lane. A Lending Library was opened in 1858, and newspapers and periodicals were supplied in 1860. In 1862 the Library was removed to the new rooms at the Guildhall, and in 1875 a Branch Library was started in Barnwell, another at the Mill Road in 1891, and a reading room in the New Town in 1907. Over a quarter of a million of books were issued from the Libraries in 1923.

In Chapter XIV I have anticipated the history of the revival of the Perse School in the first half of the nineteenth century. The constitution given to it by the scheme of 1836 provided it with opportunity, but only in 1864 did it find in Frederick Heppenstall, who became its Master in that year, a man to take advantage of its opportunity. In the eleven years of his Headship the school was much increased in numbers and efficiency. But it was long hampered by lack of means, since the fees were so low that it was not possible to provide a sufficient staff of masters in the variety of subjects of modern education. As University residents were for the most part unmarried the boys were almost all of them sons of Town parents, and until Heppenstall's appointment the school had not, and did not deserve, the confidence of Town parents. Some of its difficulties were removed by the scheme of the Endowed School Commissioners in 1873, and from its cramped site in Free School Lane it was removed to its present quarters in the Hills Road in 1890, and in 1906 it acquired an ample playing field outside the town beyond Homerton College. Under the liberal control of Dr Rouse boarding houses have been built, and the school has so greatly expanded in numbers and extended the range of its teaching that its removal to yet larger premises has become a pressing need. The school

is now conducted according to a Scheme approved
in 1910.

The Leys School was established in 1874 in connection with the Wesleyan Methodist body. It draws
its pupils from all parts and under a succession of distinguished and active Headmasters has won itself a
high place among the great schools of England.

At the beginning of the nineteenth century the
Old Schools (see Chapter XVI) provided 288 children
of the poorer classes with an education, free indeed,
but of the barest kind, the population of Cambridge
being then about 10,000. In 1924 the elementary
schools had accommodation for over 10,700 children,
out of a total population somewhat short of 60,000.

The Redistribution of Seats Act of 1885, which
limited boroughs of less than 50,000 inhabitants to a
single member, deprived the borough of one of its
representatives. Since 1295 it had regularly returned
its two members, except for a short period in Commonwealth days, when it was deprived of one of them.

In the Award Act of 1856 a lingering latency of
distrust between the academic and oppidan corporations
was shown in the clause precluding members of the
University from being registered as electors of the
Borough or being enrolled as burgesses, and exempting
them from municipal and parochial office. By the
Local Government Act of 1888 the University became
entitled to two aldermen and six councillors to represent
it on the Town Council.

The Guildhall was much enlarged and improved in
1862: municipal offices and a police court were added
to it in 1896. The Police Station and Fire Brigade
Station were built in 1901, at a cost of £16,000. The
Corn Exchange, the largest public building in Cambridge
was erected in 1876, at a cost of £20,000. A fine
County Hall, deserving of a better site than Hobson
Street, was opened in 1914. The Cattle Market
was laid out in 1885: on the acquisition of the site and

PLAN OF CAMBRIDGE

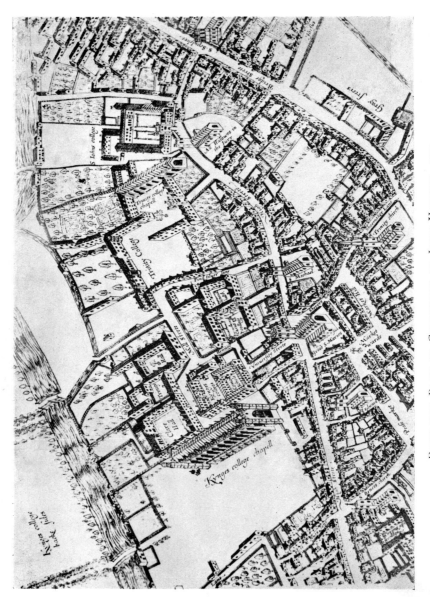

FROM THE PLAN OF CAMBRIDGE BY JOHN HAMOND, 1592

its equipment £19,000 were expended. There had been no Cattle Market before 1754: afterwards the Market Place was the place of sale, but since 1842 it had been at Pound Hill.

The main drainage scheme, carried out in 1895, cost £150,000; previously the River had carried all the drainage of the town. Considering its imperfections in the matter of drainage and water supply, Cambridge in the past was a comparatively healthy town. It suffered, indeed, from 'Cambridge fever,' apparently typhoid, in 1815, but it escaped the cholera epidemic of 1831. Plague never revisited the place after the visitation of 1665-6, and in 1783 the pesthouses on Coldham's Common were taken down and the materials sold. State Hygiene was not so much as dreamt of until the latter half of the nineteenth century, when attention was drawn to it not so much by the miseries of the poor as by the consequent pressure on the rates. Burials within town limits were not prohibited until 1852. Cambridge was in advance of the time when it opened a cemetery, next the Histon Road, in 1842, and another, near the Mill Road, in 1848. Views of Cambridge churches made in the earlier part of last century show the churchyard soil, behind brick walls, piled high above the level of the street. From time to time the earth was levelled and the surface soil was scattered on the Town Green westward of the river. At the present time Cambridge is among the healthiest of the larger towns of England, not excepting places known as 'health resorts,' such as Brighton, Bournemouth and Cheltenham. Its death rate, 11·4 per thousand, compares favourably with the sister towns, Oxford (12·75), Norwich (12·5), Ipswich (12·1).

Under the powers of the Local Government Boards Act of 1911 the area of the borough was extended by the inclusion of 300 acres from the parish of Cherryhinton, 167 from Grantchester, 495 from Trumpington, and 1300 from the Urban District of Chesterton. At the time the population of the added districts was: Chesterton 11,330, the other parishes 4455. Three new wards formed from Chesterton and one from the other parishes were at the same time added to the existing wards: each ward is represented on the Town Council by an alderman and three councillors. The area of the borough, thus extended, contains 5497 acres. The population in 1911 was 55,812, and in 1921 had increased to 59,262. The growth of the town in recent years has been mainly in the parts added from Chesterton and Grantchester. As in other towns, the tendency of the residential population is to diminish in the central parts.

Last scenes of all in the eventful history of Cambridge are of War, Victory and a thereafter which is yet in the disclosing. The part which the Town played in the vindication of England's honour and of English freedom is not dissociable from the steadfastness of the Shire. Of the thousands who, quitting Cambridgeshire homes, passed through the fiery furnace of 1914–1918, an altogether worthy and dignified memorial stands where the Station Road meets the Hills Road—the young warrior, physically weary, but resolutely striding to the far goal on which his gaze is set. The names of the fathers, husbands, sons and lovers who bade their last farewell to all that Cambridge held most dear to them must be sought not in Cambridge, but in the Minster of Cambridgeshire. On the walls of the N. transept chapel at Ely their names are recorded for after ages to read. The place is appropriate. Hard by, in Bishop West's chapel, lie the bodies of Brihtnoth and his brave company who died for English liberty in the fight at Maldon, almost a thousand years (A.D. 991) before Ely commemorated another generation of the same valiant mettle.

In the year of grace, 1925, when this page is written, exactly twelve centuries and a half have passed away

since the historic visit of the Ely coffin-seekers to the
desolate site of Grantacaestir. The period between
the legendary foundation of Rome and its sacking by
Alaric falls short of this expanse of time by nearly a
full century, and whereas A.D. 409 saw the Eternal
City in the throes of dissolution, of Cambridge it may
be securely said that the historian of its Decline and
Fall is, as yet, unborn. Transposing past into future
tense and record into prophecy, I conclude with the
tribute, paid eight centuries ago, by the chronicler,
Henry of Huntingdon :

**Dum Angli regnabunt laus Cantebrigiae
splendide florebit.**

Index